Fulfilling the Dream of Mankind

EIR Contents

www.larouchepub.com Volume 44, Number 48, December 1, 2017

Cover This Week

FULFILLING THE DREAM OF MANKIND

These presentations are edited unofficial informal transcripts and/or edited versions of speakers prepared texts.

FULFILLING THE DREAM OF MANKIND

Nov. 25-26, 207, Bad Soden/Taunus, Germany

Preliminary Conference program

(subject to last-minute changes)

SATURDAY, NOV. 25, 10 A.M.-6 P.M.

MUSICAL OPENING: Mo Li Hua (Jasmin Flower),Chinese Folk Song—Arr. Benjamin Lylloff
Schiller Institute Chorus; 1st Violin: Caroline Hartmann; 2nd Violin: Odile Mojon; Viola: Claudio Celani; Cello: Athil Hamdan; Conductor: Benjamin Lylloff

CONFERENCE KEYNOTE
- The New Silk Road, a New Model for International Relations
  Helga Zepp-LaRouche, President and Founder, Schiller Institute

PANEL I: The Earth's Next 50 Years

- KEYNOTE: President Xi's Perspective for the Year 2050 and the Perspective of African Development
  Prof. He Wenping, Chinese Academy of Social Sciences, Director of African Studies, Beijing
- Integration of Egypt's Transportation Plans 2030 with the New Silk Road Project
  Dr. Saad Mohamed Mahmoud Elgioshy, former Transport Minister, Egypt

- The Trump Administration—Impending Economic Policies and Media Discord
  George Lombardi, former Social Media Consultant to President Trump
- A Future for Europe After the Euro
  Marco Zanni, Member of the Economic and Monetary Committee, European Parliament

13:00-14:00   LUNCH BREAK

PANEL II: The Need for Europe to Cooperate With China in the Industrialization of Africa and the Middle East; Transaqua as the Rosetta Stone of the Continent's Transformation

- Extending the New Silk Road to Southwest Asia and Africa: A Vision of an Economic Renaissance
  Hussein Askary, Schiller Institute, Southwest Asia Coordinator, Stockholm
- Italy-China Alliance for Transaqua
  Franco Persio Bocchetto, Foreign Director, Bonifica S.p.A., Italy

- The Need for Europe to Cooperate with China in the Industrialization of Africa
  Mehreteab Mulugeta Haile, General Consul of the Federal Democratic Republic of Ethiopia, Frankfurt am Main

- Egypt's 2030 Mega-Projects: Investment Opportunities for Intermodal and Multimodal Connectivity
  Mrs. Moni Abdullah, Executive Manager of Pyramids International, Cairo

8 P.M. CLASSICAL CONCERT

SUNDAY, NOV. 26, 2017—10 A.M.—6 P.M.

Note: Panels III and IV will be covered in the Dec. 8 issue of EIR.

PANEL III: Europe as the Continent of Poets, Thinkers, and Inventors, or Sidelined at the Rear of Strategic Developments? An Optimistic Vision for the Future of Europe

- KEYNOTE: What Europe Should Contribute to the New World Paradigm
  Jacques Cheminade, former Presidential Candidate, France

- China's Initiative: From the Doom of Self-Destruction, to Prosperity and Progress: A View from Ukraine
  Dr. Natalia Vitrenko, Doctor of Economics, MP (1994-2002), Chairwoman of the Progressive Socialist Party of Ukraine

- One Belt, One Road—An Opportunity for Development in the Western Balkans
  Dr. Jasminka Simic, Author and Journalist, Ph.D., Research Fellow, Editor-Journalist of the Radio-Television of Serbia, Belgrade, Serbia

- Bulgaria's Contribution to the B&R Initiative in the Context of the Geopolitical State of the Balkans
  Prof. Mariana Tian, Institute for Historical Studies, Bulgarian Academy of Sciences

13:00-14:00   LUNCH BREAK

MUSICAL OPENING: Ganymed, Franz Schubert (Text: Goethe)
  Leena Malkki, Sweden—Soprano; Werner Hartmann—Piano

- New Horizons for Cyprus
  Kathryn Alexander Theodotou, Principal of Highgate Hill Solicitors in London and of Alexandrou Theodotou LLC in Cyprus, Chair of Anglo-Hellenic and Cypriot Law Association

- China's Belt and Road Initiative and Its Long-Term Impact on African Countries
  Dr. (Cand.) Alexander Demissie, Founding Director, The China Africa Advisory

PANEL IV: The System We Live in is Not Earthbound— Future Technologies and Scientific Breakthroughs (Transportation, Thermonuclear Fusion, International Cooperation in Space Research)

- KEYNOTE: The Scientific Method of LaRouche
  Jason Ross, Science Advisor, Schiller Institute, U.S.A.

- Energy Transition—from Bad to Worse
  Prof. Dr. Helmut Alt, University of Applied Sciences (Fachhochschule), Aachen

- Current Situation of High Temperature Gas-Cooled Reactor in China
  Wentao Guo, Paul Scherrer Institute, Switzerland

CONCLUDING DISCUSSION

The New Silk Road: A New Model For International Relations

Helga Zepp-LaRouche is the Founder and President of the Schiller Institute. This is an edited transcript of her presentation to the Nov. 25-26, 2017 Schiller Institute Conference, "Fulfilling the Dream of Mankind."

Ladies and gentlemen, I want to welcome you to this conference of the Schiller Institute. There are many honored people in the audience, whom we will introduce in the course of the event. But let me just greet especially the Consul General of Ethiopia, Mr. Mehreteab Mulugeta Haile.

Let me start with an idea of Gottfried Wilhelm Leibniz. He said that we are actually living in the best of all possible worlds. This is a very fundamental ontological conception. It's the idea that we are living in a developing universe, that what makes the universe the best of all those possible is its tremendous potential for development. And it is created in such a way, that every great evil challenges an even greater good to come into being.

I think when we are talking about the New Silk Road and the tremendous changes which have occurred in the world, especially in the last four years, it is actually exactly that principle which is working. Because it was the absolute, manifest lack of development under the old world order, which caused the impulse of China and the spirit of the New Silk Road to catch on, so that now many nations of the world are absolutely determined to have development, which will give a better life to all of their people.

Helga Zepp-LaRouche

Now, I think that the New Silk Road is a typical example of an idea whose time has come; and once an idea becomes a material reality in that way, it becomes a physical force in the universe. I personally have had the chance to see the evolution of this idea, which in many senses really started with this great gentleman—my husband, Lyndon LaRouche, who many decades ago—almost half a century ago—had the idea of a just new world economic order. This then became more manifest in the 1970s, then in the 1980s—but especially in 1991, when the Soviet Union disintegrated, this idea of creating a just new world economic order became very prominent.

I personally had the chance to see how it spread, after Xi Jinping announced the New Silk Road in 2013 in Kazakhstan. I visited China in 2014, and at that point there were still only a very few officials discussing it. But then it spread very rapidly. There were industrial fairs in all the cities of China; there were hundreds of international symposia; the BRICS countries started to join in the same spirit, as did the Shanghai Cooperation Organization; altogether, more than 100 large nations and international organizations joined in support. This was evident in the Belt and Road Forum this past May, where 29 heads of state spoke and 110 nations participated. Then I think the determination of the Chinese people to effect a new world economic order was consolidated in a completely new way at the 19th Congress of the Communist Party of China in October.

China International Industry Fair in Shanghai, Nov. 7, 2017.

The Optimism in China

This has generated a completely optimistic perspective. Xi Jinping announced that China will be a country in which poverty is completely eradicated by the year 2020. I think that is wonderful! And it is absolutely to be believed, because China has had an incredible economic miracle, in which it lifted 700 million people out of poverty. China now has only 42 million poor people left, so why should it not succeed in totally eliminating poverty by the year 2020? By 2035, China is to be a great modern country of socialism with Chinese characteristics, which in my view means predominantly Confucian characteristics. And by 2050, China will be—according to Xi Jinping—"a great modern country of socialism with Chinese characteristics, prosperous, strong, democratic, culturally advanced, harmonious, and beautiful."

So, the Chinese people are to be happier, and have safer and healthier lives by that time. But also, the peoples of the other countries of the world are to have better, healthier, and happier lives.

Now the Chinese media announce very proudly that this is a grand vision for the future. A new era has dawned. Xinhua wrote that "China will make a new and greater contribution to the noble cause of peace and development for all of humanity." Well, it is very easy for the Chinese people to understand that, because the whole country is already united around this mission. The spirit of the New Silk Road has also caught on in the 70-plus countries that are cooperating. There are many people in the West who have also understood that, either because they have investments in China, or

because they know that the New Silk Road is the largest infrastructure program in history. It is already now twelve or maybe even twenty times larger than the Marshall Plan was in the postwar period, but without its military connotation. It is creating total enthusiasm among all those who understand this project.

The Opponents in the West

But of course, there are also those in the West who are completely opposed. Right now, a fight is going on between the old paradigm of geopolitics and the New Paradigm of the one humanity. The representatives of the old paradigm say, "Oh, what Xi Jinping is saying is just empty propaganda. The real intention of the Chinese is to replace the United States as the hegemon. Xi Jinping is a dictator. He just wants a system that is a threat to the Western model of market-oriented democracy, and therefore, it is bad."

The President of the EU Commission, Jean-Claude Juncker, even went so far as to explain, in his so-called "State of the Union" address, that the EU fully intends to block Chinese investments in Europe under whatever pretext. There are many think-tanks like MERICS or the Rhodium Group, which see the New Silk Road only as a geopolitical challenge. *Der Spiegel* magazine of last week had a big cover story with Chinese letters on the cover—*"Xing Lai!"* which means "Wake Up!"—and an article about the awakening giant, writing that when Trump went to China just two weeks ago, he kowtowed; that this was his farewell speech, handing over the leadership of the world! That the West must urgently wake up and unite against a rising China, that the Chinese achievements are a threat to the values and the system of the West.

Now, isn't this funny? One day the headlines say that the collapse of the Chinese banks and the Chinese economy will trigger a world financial collapse—but the next day, the same papers write that China is about to take over the world.

Western Elites Unable to Reflect

Obviously, some of these critics are completely freaked out about the fact that the old order is very clearly not working—the idea that you can have a unipolar world and geopolitical control based on the An-

German weekly, Der Spiegel, *calls for the West to wake up to the alleged threat from China. Xing lai is a Chinese expression meaning "wake up."*

glo-American special relationship in the tradition of Churchill and Truman in the postwar period, and what the neo-cons started to build after the collapse of the Soviet Union. As you can see in the revolt against the system: whether it's Brexit or the defeat of Hillary Clinton in the U.S. election, the "no" to the referendum in Italy, or the pitiful collapse of the "Jamaica" coalition talks in Germany. The talks collapsed because none of the participating parties had any vision for the future, or any substantive ideas.

So, there is no comprehension among these parties of the rapidly changing strategic alignment going on in the world. The common denominator of all of these phenomena is that the Western, neo-liberal, left-liberal establishment is completely unable, *and unwilling*, to reflect on the causes of the demise of this Western system, which are: The absolutely ridiculous income gap, where eight individuals have as much wealth as half of the rest of humanity, while the gap between rich and poor is increasing in every country; the policy of regime change, of color revolution; and the abysmal situation of the refugee crisis. Also, people have seen that what we have been fighting for, for literally centuries, in terms of civil rights, has almost vanished without discussion. There is total surveillance by the NSA and the GCHQ—the British secret service.

Western values of democracy are in shambles. If the Democratic Party leadership decides one year before the party convention who the candidate will be, and then manipulates the election against Bernie Sanders for a year—that is not a happy picture of democracy. There is the collusion of the Democratic Party in the United States with British intelligence and MI6 to invent Russia-gate against Trump. There is the collusion of Obama's heads of intelligence against the elected President of the United States.

If you look at the famous human rights of the West, well, even the UN Human Rights Commission has denounced what the Troika [IMF, European Commission, and European Central Bank] has been doing in countries such as Greece—completely violating human rights. There is a deafening silence concerning the genocide in Yemen, conducted by the British and the Saudis. The way the EU has been treating the refugees has also been called a human rights violation by the United Nations.

When these people criticize China, what you can see is that they are projecting their own intentions and viewpoints onto China and the New Silk Road. These people in the West who are attacking China, cannot imagine the existence of a government which is truly devoted to the common good and a harmonious development of all people, because they think that the world is a zero-sum game—that if one wins, the other has to lose, and that they have to control the rules in order to be able to rig the game in their favor. If you can't do that, you are a loser.

This all leads to very absurd conclusions. For example, in 1995, Lester Brown, who was the President of the Earth Policy Institute, had a big scare story, "Who Will Feed China?" saying that the growing number of people in China will mean a growing demand for food, which will overstretch demand on the food supply in the world. This is nothing but the old Malthusian idea that the number of people will grow more quickly than the amount of food. Now if you look at China today, they can perfectly well feed 1.4 billion people—and I can assure you, with excellent food. Many countries would be envious to have such good food—like the British, for example. Right now China is producing 30% of the world's economic growth.

New Silk Road Reaches Africa

So, the reality is quite different from what the Western media portray.

In 2014, we published a study called *The New Silk*

Xinhua/Dan Hang

Panama President Juan Carlos Varela (L) and China Foreign Minister Wang Yi inaugurate China's embassy in Panama City, Panama, Sept 17, 2017.

Road Becomes the World Land-Bridge. That is exactly what is happening. What started with just the old Silk Road line between China and Europe, is now very quickly developing into six major development corridors.

Freight trains already run from China to different European locations over 40 rail lines every week. The 16+1 countries—that is, the Eastern and Central European countries and China—are having a conference right now in Budapest. They are completely on-board the collaboration with the New Silk Road. There is a new Balkans Silk Road. The President of Panama was just in China after Panama switched its diplomatic relations from Taiwan; now they are allied with the mainland. The President of Panama said that all of Latin America will join the New Silk Road, and that this is not directed against the United States, because the United States is also invited to join.

The New Silk Road has reached Africa, and there it has changed the mood in an unbelievable way. There is now a total sense of optimism.

But the most important shift, of course, is that of the United States, and of the relationship between China and the United States. The result of the recent trip of President Trump and his two-day state visit to China, is obviously the most consequential. Because if the two largest economies of the world have a good relationship, then prospects for world peace are moving in a very positive direction. Remember that the policy of Obama was the so-called "Pivot to Asia" and the TPP—which was the idea of the encirclement of China and

exclusion of China. There is still an element of geopolitics, so we have to watch whenever the term "Indo-Pacific" is used, which is the idea of making Japan, Australia, and India a counterweight to China.

But a major breakthrough occurred when Trump visited China, where Xi Jinping gave him the most unbelievable reception—what Xi called "state visit-plus-plus." Remarkably, he closed down the Forbidden City for the day. The Forbidden City is the world's largest complex of palaces, where the Chinese emperors had lived since the 15th Century. It's incredibly beautiful; it's majestic, it's really breathtaking. So, Xi Jinping used an entire day to give Trump and the First Lady a course in Chinese history. They had a beautiful gala dinner; they had three Beijing operas. I want to read you some of the statements made by President Trump, which I think you need to hear because the Western media naturally will not report a single word of it.

'Proud Spirits of America and China'

Trump, commenting the next day on his reception, said:

> Yesterday, we visited the Forbidden City, which stands as a proud symbol of China's rich culture and majestic spirit. Your nation is a testament to thousands of years of vibrant, living history.
>
> And today, it was a tremendous honor to be greeted by the Chinese delegation right here at the Great Hall of the People. This moment in history presents both our nations with an incredible opportunity to advance peace and prosperity alongside other nations all around the world. In the words of a Chinese proverb, "We must carry forward the cause and forge ahead into the future." I am confident that we can realize this wonderful vision, a vision that will be so good and, in fact, so great for both China and the United States.
>
> Though we come from different places and faraway lands, there is much that binds the East and West. Both of our countries were built by people of great courage, strong culture, and a desire to trek across the unknown into great danger. But they overcame.

The people of the United States have a very deep respect for the heritage of your country and the noble traditions of its people. Your ancient values bring past and future together into the present. So beautiful.

It is my hope that the proud spirits of the American and Chinese people will inspire our efforts to achieve a more just, secure, and peaceful world, a future worthy of the sacrifices of our ancestors, and the dreams of our children.

Now I am sure that that is not what you read in *Bildzeitung* about Trump, nor does it ever report what President Trump is actually doing.

The Chinese Ambassador to Washington, Cui Tiankai, recently made the point that there were sixteen times in world history when a rising country surpassed the country that had been dominant up to that point. In twelve cases it led to a war, while in four cases the rising country took over peacefully. He said that China wants neither of those outcomes, but that China wants to have a completely different system of a win-win relationship of equality and respect for one another.

It's clear that the most important question, strategically, if you think about it, is to avoid the so-called "Thucydides trap." That was the tension, the rivalry between Athens and Sparta in the Fifth Century BC, which led to the Peloponnesian War and the demise of ancient Greece. I think nobody in his right mind could wish that this occur today between the United States and China in the age of thermonuclear weapons—and therefore, we should all be extremely happy that Trump and Xi Jinping have developed this very important relationship.

I stuck my neck out in the United States in February of this year, by saying that if President Trump manages to get a good relationship between the United States and China, and the United States and Russia, then he will go down in history as one of the greatest Presidents of the United States. Of course everybody was completely freaked out, because that is not the picture people are supposed to have about Trump. But I think if you look at what is happening, you will see that Trump is well on the way to accomplishing exactly that.

Trump came back from this Asia trip with $253 billion worth of deals with China. I watched the Nov. 13 press conference of the Governor of West Virginia, Jim Justice, who said that now, because of China, there is hope in West Virginia. West Virginia is a totally depressed state; it has high unemployment and a drug epi-

Governor.wv.gov

Gov. Jim Justice discussing at a press conference on Nov. 13, 2017, the $83 billion investment deal between West Virginia and the China Energy Investment Corporation.

demic. But he said that now we can have value-added production, and we will have a bright future. So the spirit of the New Silk Road has even caught on in West Virginia.

Obviously the United States has an enormous demand for infrastructure, especially now, after the destruction wrought by the hurricanes. Just to restore what has been destroyed will require $200 billion, without even talking about disaster prevention. So, this is all on a good path for China to invest in the infrastructure of the United States, and vice versa, for U.S. firms to cooperate in projects of the Belt and Road Initiative.

Putin's Grand Design

There is a strategic realignment caused by all of this. The relationship between Presidents Xi and Putin is the best in history. They have developed a close friendship, and the integration of the New Silk Road and the Eurasian Economic Union is now quickly expanding.

In a separate, but nevertheless related development, there was a historic visit of Syria's President Bashar al-Assad to Sochi, Russia, just now, to meet with Putin. What actually happened there was diametrically opposite to what you would read in the media, which says, of course, "the dictator Putin and the horrible Assad." But what happened was the opposite. Putin introduced Assad to the Russian military leadership, and Assad thanked them for having saved Syria. Remember that when, more than two years ago, Putin decided that the Russian military would intervene in Syria to defeat ISIS, that country was in complete disarray. It was hopeless. Al-Qaeda and ISIS were winning. But now,

Russia President Vladimir Putin (center) and Syrian President Bashar al-Assad (left of Putin) meeting with senior Russian military officials in Russia, Nov. 20, 2017.

they are militarily defeated and the reconstruction can actually begin—and Assad invited the refugees to return to help in the reconstruction of the country.

And the Silk Road will also be extended into Afghanistan, into Iraq, and hopefully all the other nearby countries.

This is a grand design of Putin, which involves the Astana process. He is integrating Turkey, Iran, and Jordan, and *even* trying to get Saudi Arabia onto a different track. We were already pushing the idea of extending the New Silk Road into Southwest Asia a long time ago. By 2012, we had a conference of the Schiller Institute, also in Frankfurt like today's, where we said that the only way to stop terrorism and unleash development and peace in the Middle East, is for all the big neighbors—Russia, China, India, Iran, the United States, and also European countries—to join hands in its development.

This is now a concrete possibility, because of the Russian military intervention and the Chinese extension of the Silk Road. In this context, the relationship between Putin and Trump has also gotten onto a much better track: In the aftermath of the Assad visit, Putin and Trump had a 90-minute telephone discussion; and people in Russia on various levels—in the Duma and in the Federation Council—afterwards expressed great optimism that the relationship between Russia and the United States can now become much more fruitful and better.

Think about it—because I know that almost everything I am saying goes against all that you hear in the Western media. But think: From whom does the motion for peace and development come? Is it coming from those who attack Putin, Xi, and Trump? And from those who support Obama? It's obviously time for people to rethink what the Western viewpoint is on all of these matters, or to change the glasses through which they look at the world.

Besides the change in the relations between the United States and China—and that in Southwest Asia—the biggest change for the better as a result of the New Silk Road, is in Africa. China has invested in Africa.

In railways, it has built a railway from Djibouti to Addis Ababa; it is building other railways from Kenya, and they are supposed to go to Rwanda. They are building hydropower dams and industrial parks. Especially in the last four years, the outlook of most Africans has completely changed, because they see, for the first time, that after suppression by colonialism and the denial of development through the IMF conditionalities, there is a possibility to truly develop the continent. They do not want to be lectured any longer about good governance, human rights, and democracy, with no development—which is what the Europeans normally offer, but they want to treated as equal partners.

Lyndon LaRouche's Vision for Africa

Let me give tribute to the person who had that vision for African development more than 40 years ago—again, my sweet husband. [applause] He wrote in 1980, as a supplement to the OAU's *Lagos Plan of Action*, a book-length paper with the title "Stop Club of Rome Genocide in Africa! Critical Comments Appended to the Lagos Plan of Action."

There he laid out a beautiful vision, a grand design for the development of Africa, based on the LaRouche scientific method of physical economy, which in turn is based on Leibniz and Alexander Hamilton's credit policy, but LaRouche of course has added very much to that. He said, "The competent conception of economic processes flows originally from a moral principle, which is immediately accessible to any sane adult or adolescent in any part of the world, however literate or illiterate. To make my mortal individual existence of some value, how do I develop and inform my practice to produce something of benefit for the development of generations to come?"

Lyn defines economic science as an inseparable facet of science, usefully called "statecraft," which includes the development of law and the cultural advancement of the people—the development of the individual to master the lawful principles of the composition of the universe. He presented a total counterposition to that of the Club of Rome, with its "appropriate technologies" and "sustainable development"—which is just another word for no development. He proposed to upgrade the labor force continuously to higher modes of production, by changing the proportions of employment from rural to urban productive occupations, using continuously higher energy-flux densities in the mode of production.

He took as a reference point for the development of Africa, the development of the United States, and showed how, for example, in the United States at the end of the 18th Century, 98% of the people worked in agriculture. Today it is less than 4%, obviously producing much more food than at the time. This exemplifies the way for Africa to go, including the development of roads, canals, and railroads; the specialization of farmers; the increase of productivity and income in agriculture and industry; a shift away from labor-intensive to capital-intensive modes of production; and better education—all amounting to the development of the power of the population to produce material alterations of nature with an increasing potential relative population-density and at higher energy-flux densities.

He said, "The development of Africa must be directed to what nations of Africa are to become by the year 2000 and 2020." This was written in 1980, namely, two generations ago. He said, "The conception needed is one of the development of the productive powers of the entire population, over the development period spanning two generations." Apart from basic infrastructure—meaning a continental system of rail, waterways, and highways—he proposed a string of new cities of 250,000 to a maximum of 2 million inhabitants, where at the core of each new city would be an

Stop Club of Rome Genocide in Africa!

Critical Comments Appended to The Lagos Plan of Action

Lyndon H. LaRouche, Jr.
and the
Executive Intelligence Review

New Benjamin Franklin House Publishing Company/New York

Released by Lyndon LaRouche, April 28, 1981.

educational complex of pedagogical museums, libraries, cultural centers, parks, and teaching and research institutions, including medical science and research institutions.

He proposed a connected system of rapid transport for persons and freight, and low-cost transition from one mode of transport to another. He envisioned inner-city distribution of freight from warehouses in the city to stores, with daily deliveries of perishable goods such as foodstuffs. And around the core of the educational complex, then residential, industrial, and commercial areas would be developed.

Productive, Beautiful Cities in Africa

The cities were not only supposed to be functionally well designed, but beautiful, using the principles of Platonic ratios in architecture. Utilizing, for example, those methods used in Gothic cathedrals, or in the architecture of the Golden Renaissance of Italy. It included the idea of having many trees and flora, so that people would be happy and the climate would be moderated.

He said, "The essential thing which the citizens of such a city must experience over the course of the city's gradual completion, is a sense of ongoing progress of perfection." To aid this process, there should be technology transfer from the developed countries, financed by grants. He made the correct point that technology transfer from Europe and the United States to Africa would stimulate the economy in the exporting nations and increase their tax income, and that the developing countries receiving grants would become the next generation's customers for purchasing on a credit basis. The exporting nations would develop prosperous customers for tomorrow, and have an accelerated turnover of capital stocks, and thus those exporting countries would increase their productivity, and therefore their national and per-capita wealth.

Now, that is obviously completely the opposite of what the IMF did, which lured countries into the "debt trap" which was quite dramatically exposed by John Perkins in his book, *Confessions of an Economic Hit Man.*

Xinhua/Li Baishun

Ethiopia-Djibouti railway operational test on Oct. 3, 2016, Africa's first modern electrified railway—built by Chinese firms.

Now, Lyn [LaRouche], on the other side, said that, "The technology-exporting nations must seek those portions of the labor force in the developing nations, which can be upgraded immediately to productive employment, using the most advanced technologies embodied in the capital stock to be exported from the industrialized nations. That labor force is able to assimilate the advanced technologies, and that must be expanded. It requires methods of promoting the development potentials of the population on a large scale, so the investment in infrastructure and the development of the population has to occur at the same time." He said, "Every infant born in any part of the world, has the potential for the development of his or her mental powers to the level sufficient for a direct, competent use of modern technology. It is that potential development which is the only source of wealth. That development is a creditworthy asset in the eyes of a truly prudent lender."

Citizens Become Artists

So what occurs at the point where economic development will have absorbed most of the population of the world? By that time, we must have an increase in the rate of development of technology, such that we no longer depend on the expansion of the economy in scale. When that transition to a new world economic order has been completed, we will have more and more members of society living and working as artists; as "golden souls," as Plato describes them; as "beautiful souls" as Schiller terms it; as *junzi*, the Confucian idea of the noble man; or the people living on the level of Paradise in Dante's *Commedia*; or, as Vladimir Verna-

dsky says, that the noösphere—that part of the physical universe which is dominated by creative activity of man—will take over more and more of the biosphere.

Actually, what is happening right now goes in this direction. What Xi Jinping has defined as a goal for 2050 for China and the rest of the world, is to lead better and happier lives, with poverty having been eradicated and people being able to devote their lives to meaningful purposes. This actually goes very much in this direction.

Is this realistic? I can practically can hear the howls of protest of the neo-liberals and neo-cons alike, in the West. "What about Western values? What about our freedom? What about democracy?"—or better, "market-conformed democracy," as German Chancellor Mrs. Merkel likes to put it.

We had better reflect where these values have gotten us in Europe. Europe is completely disunited. We are faced with a financial crisis, worse than that of 2008, about to erupt. The EU has just completed guidelines eliminating the possibility for the separation of the banks, a Glass-Steagall type of separation which China has just reconfirmed. The right-wing movements are rising, and the refugee crisis has caused the reputation of Europe to go down the drain completely in the world. There is a very dangerous anti-immigration sentiment.

The entire social and political fabric of Europe is disintegrating. Because Europe, in its present form of the European Union, is like a giant Tower of Babel, attempting an amalgamation of cultures, languages, and histories that leads to ever more frictions between supranational integration and the self-interest of these nations of Europe. Not to even mention the government crisis in Germany, which is the worst since 1949, since the founding of the German Federal Republic.

Leibniz's Proposals Were Analogous

This is not the first time that Europe has been in bad shape. This was addressed by Gottfried Wilhelm Leibniz in a policy memorandum of 1670, in which he named the challenges of his time—"in badly established trade and manufacturing; in an entirely debased currency; in the uncertainty of law and the delay of all legal actions; in worthless education … in an increase in atheism, in our morals, which are, as it were, infected by a foreign plague; in the bitter strife of religions; all of which … weaken us, and, … may in the end completely ruin us…." So, that was the situation Leibniz saw.

This was still in the aftermath of 150 years of religious war in Europe, when he came up with the idea that the solution was a merger of the Chinese ancient natural theology and European culture. He called it a beautiful coincidence that the two most developed cultures in the world, are like two poles reaching hands across between Europe and China. By creating a common exchange between them, civilization could reach the next, superior stage in human history.

In the preface of his *Novissima Sinica* (The Latest from China), he expressed this intention. Leibniz very closely followed all the news from China. He engaged in a very lively dialogue with many of the Jesuit missionaries, who informed him on all of the developments in science and the famous "Rites Controversy," in which he sided with people of Matteo Ricci's view, saying that there was a strong affinity between Confucianism and Christianity.

He said that Confucianism has much more to offer than any other known belief system of his time. He said, "We need the Chinese to send missionaries to Europe, so that we can learn from them the natural religion that we have almost lost." He proposed an exchange of cultural ambassadors, which for his time was a very modern conception. He said, "There is in China a public morality, admirable in certain regards, conjoined to a philosophical doctrine, or rather a natural theology venerable by its antiquity, established and authorized for about 3,000 years, long before the philosophy of the Greeks."

Statue of Gottfried Leibniz.

Matteo Ricci (left) and Xu Guangqi.

For Leibniz, the affinity of Confucius and Christianity, despite all differences in culture, proved that humanity has the universal characteristic of reason. The fact that the Kangxi Emperor and he—Leibniz—studied the same mathematical solutions, proved for him the universal character of human reason and the human species. In Chinese philosophy, he emphasized that the notion of the *li* refers to the supreme order of the universe, in which harmony exists if each being exercises its lawful function in its proper place. And together with the notion of *ren*, which approximates the Christian notion of agape—love—the Chinese Confucians use different terminologies and different conceptions, but they have analogy with, and affinity to what Leibniz describes in his *Monadology*.

According to Leibniz, "God has created the universe by the way of a pre-stabilized harmony, where the realm of the spiritual and the material world, the soul and the body are in total correspondence. This is so, because God—in His divine anticipation—has created the material and spiritual substance in such an ordered way and with such a precision, that even if they follow their own lawfulness embedded in their nature, nevertheless there is such a cohesion as if there existed between them, a reciprocal inference. And as if God, apart from His general contribution, were to act concretely in each single instant. Each monad, each uniform substance, reflects in germ the entire universe at large. But they only relate to each other because they take part in the absolute being of God."

Leibniz and Xi Jinping

Once one understands this inner cohesion between Chinese

ancient philosophy, especially in the Confucian expression, and the idea of Leibniz, it is no surprise that he not only recognized the affinity, but concretely thought a reciprocal exchange of the two cultures would merge into a superior, more advanced level of civilization. Among Leibniz's plans for this project were the creation of a world language, for which he thought the Chinese language and script were most appropriate; the creation of a world academy of sciences, where Chinese and Western scientists would work together; and the creation of a world citizenship, which would allow every human being to absorb all cultures of the world.

He envisioned the future role of Russia in mediating between China and the West, and the development of Siberia in relation to the development of Northern Africa. And Peter the Great, with whom he was in contact, in 1712 ordered the expedition of Vitus Jonassen Bering, for whom the Bering Strait has been named.

Further, he advocated the comparative study of languages to find the common origin of human language, which was later pursued by philologists such as Humboldt and others. He proposed a chronology of the history of the West and China—and the only museum where I have seen that, is the museum in Taipei, where you have a beautiful exhibition where you see above the history of China, and below what happened parallel in the Western culture—which gives you a completely different way of thinking about universal history.

He also pioneered the binary system, which became the basis for computers and the like, and found evidence of its prior use in China. He proposed the development of a key which would make it easier to learn the Chinese language—now I think everybody who has tried to learn Chinese would be very thankful for such a key. He advocated the development of a method to teach the difference between Western and Chinese culture. He called for defining principles of a new moral code for Western statesmen and politicians, but also to guide the behavior of the ordinary citizen—based on Confucianism. He wanted an analysis of Confucianism based on Western methods, intending to show its closeness to Western Christianity.

If you look at these plans by Leibniz, it is absolutely amazing how similar they are to what Xi Jinping is doing with the New Silk Road policy today, which has aspects of all of these plans. So why, then, in the West, are so many people having a hard time accepting an offer of a "win-win cooperation" among all nations, which would be so clearly in the interest of all people?

The CCF's Cultural Poison

Let me briefly go back to the end of World War II, to find the roots of this problem. Franklin D. Roosevelt, in his famous dialogue with Churchill in Casablanca, had pledged the end of colonialism and the help of the United States to develop the developing countries. Churchill, on the other side, said the British did not fight World War II in order to end the British Empire. Now unfortunately, Roosevelt died at a very inconvenient moment, and Truman—who was a very small man—took over the White House. Remember what Lyn always said—he was in India at the time—about how shocked the people were when Roosevelt died at that point.

So Roosevelt, who was allied with the Soviet Union in the Second World War, had gone. Churchill stepped into this vacuum, and basically then he made his famous March 1946 "Iron Curtain" speech in Fulton, Missouri, launching the Cold War.

Churchill proposed a new alliance, based on the special relationship between the United States and the British Empire, and that speech by Churchill in Fulton shifted the American view on the U.S.S.R. Then followed the Truman Doctrine in March 1947, which allowed such atrocities as Sen. Joseph McCarthy's witchhunt in America against everybody suspected of being a communist—a communist under every bed. Now this is what is happening with the anti-Trump witchhunt today.

What happened in Europe? Recently there was an amazing article in the leading German daily, the *Frankfurter Allgemeine Zeitung* (FAZ), covering an exhibition taking place in Berlin right now, on the occasion of the 50th anniversary of the scandal erupting around the Congress for Cultural Freedom (CCF).

The CCF, which lasted from 1950 to 1967, was the gigantic cultural warfare program by the CIA, which had as its aim to recruit left-wing people, communists, into an anti-Soviet Cold War. In reality, they wanted to destroy the axioms in the population which had made Franklin D. Roosevelt possible, because Wall Street had been completely freaked out about Roosevelt's implementing Glass-Steagall, about his New Deal, and his alliance with the Soviet Union. So, once they were rid of Roosevelt, Truman started, in cohesion with the British, to establish a paradigm shift in the population,

President Franklin D. Roosevelt (left) and British Prime Minister Winston Churchill holding talks in Casablanca, Morocco, Jan. 22, 1943.

using the left-liberal outlook which we have today. That is what the *FAZ* article said. It said the CIA did not plan to foster reactionary movements: Rather, they created exactly that left-liberal axiomatic outlook which is the politically correct view in Europe today.

I think that is really noteworthy to reflect upon, because that is exactly what they did in Germany through the Dulles brothers and High Commissioner [the U.S. dictator for defeated Germany] John Jay McCloy. If you look at this operation, it was huge: It involved 35 countries and 20 magazines. The CIA controlled practically every art exhibition and cultural event. In Europe, there were very few writers, poets, musicians, historians, critics, and journalists who were not connected to this project—some witting, many unwitting. It was part of the Cold War to fight for "the liberation of the human mind." The CCF acted like a cartel. It controlled the entire cultural industry and based it on the myth of a freedom-oriented outlook.

Remember, the CIA, at the same time that it pretended to be for freedom, made a coup against Mossadegh in Iran, conducted the Bay of Pigs operation against Cuba, Operation Phoenix in Vietnam, and other similar operations.

The CCF and the Frankfurt School

The cultural warfare was in part funded with money from the Marshall Plan, diverted to the CCF, but also, by altogether 170 foundations. One of the key ideologues, George Kennan, in a speech before the National War College in December 1947, developed the

strategy of the "necessary lie," which would become an essential part of U.S. foreign policy, laid down in NSC Directive 4A, and later in another directive for psychological warfare operations. This lasted for decades. So, the idea of fake news, of manipulating the population with lies, is not new, and it has not erupted only against Trump.

The aims of the CCF were very much those of the Frankfurt School. They wanted to destroy idealism and Classical culture. The Frankfurt School's Theodor Adorno, for example, argued that idealism leads to Nazism, because it leads to a radical view. That has to be rooted out; both in order to eradicate the remnants of Nazism, but also to work against the dictatorship of the Soviet Union. Adorno said, for this purpose, we have to eradicate beauty from art completely. Remember that Schiller said that art which is not beautiful is not art. And I fully agree, because art has to ennoble people and uplift their spirit, and when it's not beautiful, it does not do that.

In music, the CCF started a vicious campaign against Furtwängler; and instead of Classical composers, it pushed atonal, twelve-tone music, such as that of Alban Berg, Schoenberg, and Webern, and eradicated the idea of polyphonic harmonic composition. The famous writer, Susan Sontag, said, "We knew we expected to accept ugly music as pleasant." That is what

Berlin museum exhibit on the Congress for Cultural Freedom.

Schiller Institute.

Musical presentation at the conference.

happens when you go to the concerts—the Rheingau festivals or others—you always have Beethoven, alongside Berg and some other modern composer. You never can get a Classical concert.

They also made a list of allowed writers—including Ibsen, Shaw, O'Neill, Wilder, and Steinbeck. They forbade certain plays of Shakespeare and Kleist, and they invented the famous *Regietheater*, which is the idea that you completely destroy the Classical composition of Schiller or Shakespeare—each modern director puts his own interpretation on it, up to the point that you cannot recognize these plays any longer.

A big role was played by the Museum of Modern Art in New York, which promoted modern painting— Cubism, Futurism, Dadaism, Expressionism, abstract art, serialism, and so forth. The writer Eva Cockcroft wrote in *ArtForum* magazine, "Abstract expressionism was a weapon of the Cold War." The connection between the Cold War and this expressionism was absolutely no coincidence, because it was intended to destroy the ability of the mind to understand anything. Harry Truman—of all people—liked to go to the National Art Gallery in the United States, to see Holbein and Rembrandt. He said, "What a pure pleasure, and what a difference from our modern *Schmierfinken* [hacks], our mucky pups."

The CCF influence did not end in 1967. It ended under that name, when everything came out in a big scandal, but its influence is working to the present. This is why people have this left-liberal ideology today. This is what is behind the interventionist policy, the color revolution, the export of democracy, the "right to protect" (R2P). This is what Russian Foreign Minister Lavrov calls "the post-Christian values." He said, "Western values are no longer those values which were handed down from our grandfathers, from generation to generation. But it has been replaced by 'everything is allowed'—a complete hedonism, where freedom is misunderstood as the right of everybody to live out all their pleasures in the here and now. Do whatever you like to do."

That ugliness is what you see when you look at most movies nowadays, at the video games, the art, or youth culture, which are all characterized by a cult of ugliness. So, in that sense, the CCF has done a very successful job.

Revive Classical Culture!

So, we do have a problem in the West, a big cultural problem. There is a huge drug epidemic in the United States, out-of-control violence, mass shootings in schools almost every week, and terrorism. But the good news is that the solution to these problems is readily available. When we founded the Schiller Institute—now more than 33 years ago—we said from the beginning that a just new world economic order must be combined with a renaissance of Classical culture. This is now actually happening, because with the New Silk Road development being pursued for four years now, the world has changed already, and many countries are reviving their Classical cultures. This is why the Schiller Institute, in all our conferences, always have a concert expressing this dialogue of Classical cultures.

We obviously need a completely new set of international relations. We must overcome geopolitics, and we must have a system of relations among us with total respect for sovereignty, non-interference, respect for the different social systems, win-win cooperation in the mutual interest of all of us, and the perspective of one single humanity.

Nicholas of Cusa, who developed the method of the *Coincidentia oppositorum*, the idea of the Coincidence of Opposites, argued that the One has a higher power, a higher order of magnitude than the Many. So the idea of harmony in the macrocosm is only possible when you have the best development of all microcosms. That development must not be static or linear, but it works like a contrapuntal fugue, where each development furthers the development of the next segment, becoming unified into a higher concept of the composition.

What we have to build is a completely new set of international relations in which each nation is allowed to celebrate statecraft, meaning making possible the realization of the creative potential of all of its citizens.

This will be an interaction among nations in which each focuses on the best cultural tradition and potential of the other. China is reviving Confucianism and its philosophy of philosophical Classical culture in poetry, music, and painting.

In Europe, we must absolutely do the same. We must revive the ancient Greek Classical period, which is what Greece is actually doing: They recently had a conference in Athens of the ten oldest civilizations, and they revived exactly that spirit. In Italy, we have the Golden Renaissance; in Spain, the Andalusian renaissance and other great thinkers. In France, you have the traditions of Louis XI, Jeanne d'Arc, and the [Ecole] Polytechnique. In Germany, we have a tremendous wealth of philosophers, composers, and poets—Schiller and Beethoven. In America, we have the American Constitution, the American System of economy. All these treasures are there, and only need to be revived.

If we undo what the CCF did, revive the Classical culture of all nations, and enter a beautiful dialogue among them, mankind will experience a new renaissance and unleash the enormous creativity of the human species as never before.

So, it is very good to live at this moment in history, and contribute to make the world a better place. And it can be done, because the New Paradigm corresponds to the lawfulness of the physical universe in science, Classical art, and these principles. Neo-liberalism and left-liberalism are as outdated as Scholasticism, and will disappear, as did the scholastics debating how many angels can fit on the head of a pin. What will be asserted is the identity of the human species as *the* creative species in the universe. [applause]

Greetings to the Nov. 25-26 Schiller Conference

The Schiller Institute international conference "Fulfilling the Dreams of Mankind," convened in Germany on November 25-26, received greetings and well wishes from prominent people across the globe. The following is our first report of some of those greetings.

Yemen: Fouad Al-Ghaffari, founder of the Office for Coordination with the BRICS (Brazil, Russia, India, China and South Africa) and President of the Yemeni BRICS Youth Cabinet and presented a beautiful 15 minute video with his on-the-ground report, his greetings, and greetings from many of his associates who despite the grim circumstances in Yemen itself, are working ardently for the full LaRouche program in collaboration with the Chinese One Belt One Road (OBOR) New Silk Road initiative.

Speaking from Yemen, he opened the taped video message, telling the audience gathered in Germany, "With a great deal of pain mixed with hope, we tape this fourth message from adistance, today, Oct. 17, to greet you, the Schiller Institute, at your conference. I greet you from Sanaa International Airport. It is closed be-

Fouad Al-Ghaffari from his video greeting to the conference.

cause of Saudi aggression, prevented me from attending your conference, and also prevented tens of thousands of Yemenis from traveling for medical treatment or to pursue their education and work. This is a crime that the whole world is witnessing."

The greeting concluded with a call for, "a new chapter in the book of the new international relations," very much advanced by President Trump's visit to China. That visit, he said, holds out the hope to "replace a doctrine of international relations that brought sorrow and destruction to the world, which should not have come into existence in the first place," so that mankind can now move "from the regime-change system to the more natural system of sovereignty of nations, that are joined together around one dream of mankind."

South Africa: Dr. Kelvin Kemm, CEO of Nuclear Africa, a nuclear project management company based in Pretoria, South Africa, sent his warmest wishes for success, reminding the audience that the site of the modern Cape Town, South Africa was found by Bartholomew Diaz in 1488,

Dr. Kelvin Kemm

while pursuing the Silk Road from Portugal. "Today, he said, "on any given day, some 2,000 ships are forging through the ocean waters of South Africa, moving around the Cape of Good Hope from one end of the traditional Silk Road to the other, but by the ocean route and not the camel-train route. A vast quality of trade also moves in and out of South African ports, moving not only into the interior of South Africa, but also deep into land-locked African countries. Africa is larger than the United States, Europe, China, and India put together. It is big—really big. There is a great deal of trade potential in Africa."

African Great Lakes Region: José Mulenda Zangela sent greetings. He is the sponsor of the proposed "African Rift Border Navigable Canal" project, referred to in Swahil as *Sula ya Amani* (the face of peace). He described the project: to build a 2,000 km navigable corridor uniting Lakes Victoria, Albert, Eduard, Kivu, Tanganyika,

José Mulenda Zangela

and Malawi through canals to the Indian Ocean which would "open up" several countries in the region and promote regional and global economic integration for the benefit of an East African population of more than 200 million. This aspiration "has certainly brought us closer to the Schiller Institute, with whom we can establish the connection between the African Great Lakes Region, not only to the New Silk Road, but also and especially to the philosophy of this road, revived by Mrs. Helga Zepp-LaRouche."

France: Michel Tognini, former astronaut at the French National Center of Space Studies and former Head of the European Astronaut Center at the European Space Agency, veteran of two space flights, aboard the Soyuz in 1992, and the Space Shuttle Columbia in 1999, and an active proponent of space exploration, sent a message highlighting

Michel Tognini

the joint Russian-American initiatives in space exploration beginning in 1975. Up to the present time, he said, "The International Space Station remains an extraordinary experience that has led to considerable scientific progress in a spirit of sharing and by an exemplary peaceful cooperation. It is proof that science does not belong to one country, but to all who inhabit the earth."

"Today, this experience inspires an even more ambitious and grandiose project, that of an international village on the Moon, a scientific base called 'Moon Village.' This visionary project will have more participants than any previous project. It is now proposed by the European Space Agency and is of great interest to China and other countries. This cooperation is so admirable that, even in this time of great tension, it will succeed in bringing world political leaders together for the common goals of humanity. Our world, today unstable, is now ready to move towards peace. It requires a great mission to unite all forces towards this goal.

"Space, in its broadest sense, will be this mission."

Portugal: Fernanda Ilhé (Ph.D.), President of "New Silk Road Friends" thanked the Schiller Institute and expressed her best wishes for "very productive work" to come. She reported that Portugal was "one of the countries which joined the One Belt One Road and the 21st Century Maritime Silk Road. This initiative will change the

Fernanda Ilhé

world, as the Portuguese Maritime Silk Road did in the 15th and 16th Centuries. It doesn´t matter if the paths are from West to East or from East to West, the final outcomes will be similar: a new dimension of globalization that will change the world. The only difference will be the speed and the scale. Now, with new technologies, we can expect to share all their benefits in a more simultaneous way and on a bigger scale.

"Portuguese history and heritage has linked us to China since the 16th Century and our co-existence in Macau is seen by both countries as very positive; so the Chinese government is encouraging Portugal to have an important role in the Atlantic Road, and our geography also clearly recommends it. The Portuguese government is already negotiating with the Chinese government on projects to jointly develop, among others, the blue (maritime) economy cluster."

• **Roger Stone,** a longtime friend of President Donald Trump offered his congratulations for "your efforts to stop the regime change coup underway in the United States, against my long-time friend, President Donald J. Trump. The election of Trump signaled a desire among many Americans, from all walks of life, but especially among the 'silent majority,' for a dramatic change of direction in U.S. policy. The American people are tired of the destructive wars our elected leaders have started, which

Roger Stone

benefit only a small group of elites; they are tired of economic policies which benefit the same small group of elites; and they are sick and tired of being treated as ignorant fools by arrogant and corrupt politicians and journalists. This is not just happening in the U.S., but is part of a worldwide rebellion.

"These policies, of wars and coups, of bailouts and austerity, have caused enormous hardship and loss of lives; have added trillions of dollars of debt to our nation, our businesses, and to American families; have imposed trade deals which benefit those who ship jobs overseas, and close America's manufacturing enterprises; and have created a financial bubble which, while stealing the savings of millions and shutting down our productive industries, have also robbed our young people of a future."

• **George Lombardi**, a former executive director of the International Council for Economic Development and social media advisor to candidate Donald Trump, applauded President Trump's collaboration with Presidents Xi and Putin. He contrasted the real Trump to the horrible image of him presented by

George Lombardi

the media, comparing Trump to FDR in his 'extreme confidence' in believing that America's problems can be solved. The media which attacks Trump, he said, is "not in line with public sentiment," not reporting that there is 'tremendous popular support for Trump," from American business and American workers.

Earth's Next 50 Years

PROF. HE WENPING

The Belt and Road: China Shares Its Development with Africa and the World

Prof. He Wenping

Prof. He Wenping is the Director of African Studies at the Chinese Academy of Social Sciences in Beijing. This is an edited transcript of her address to the International Schiller Institute conference on "Fulfilling the Dream of Mankind," Nov. 25, 2017, in Bad Soden/Taunus, Germany, which she presented under the title, "President Xi's Perspective for the Year 2050 and the Perspective of African Development." Subtitles have been added.

Good morning, Ladies and Gentlemen. It is a great honor for me to be here, to join in this wonderful conference. Thank you very much, Mme. Helga Zepp-LaRouche, President and founder of the Schiller Institute, for inviting me here. I am very impressed, first of all, by this opening music, the lovely song called "The Jasmine Flower." Actually, when I hear the beautiful song, I have a kind of motivation to jump on stage, to sing together with this beautiful song. [applause]

This song I know is very famous in the Western society, seemingly like one of the Chinese dishes that is called Gong Bao Ji Ding, which I hear is also very famous in European countries, and especially in Germany. I think several years ago, when I spent my visit-ing fellowship in the German Development Institute, I had a very good friend—she's a German—she invited me to her apartment to cook this Gong Bao Ji Ding. And she followed all the procedures, how to begin doing it from the first step, second step, so it's amazing. Even me, I couldn't do that Gong Bao Ji Ding from the beginning to the end. So, we tasted that delicious dish together.

So, like founder and President Helga said, now in China, the Chinese people eat very well, but not so healthy! We have to learn how to diet now! Before, during Mao's time, we had a shortage economy, and when Deng Xiaoping made reforms and this reform, the "Opening Up," and now the Chinese can feed themselves. But, now they're learning how to eat healthily, how to do the diet. So, I want to speak over my dinner, and also do a diet in order to keep a good figure.

Today I think it's a wonderful conference theme, called "Fulfilling the Dream of Mankind." I have the honor of talking about President Xi Jinping's perspective for the year 2050, and the perspective of African development. I have been told I have 20 minutes—I hope I can finish all my slides in 20 minutes.

First, the point in China is the roadmap and this development goal of 2050; 2050 is not too much further away, it's just quickly, every year passes so quickly, so very soon we will reach 2050. His perspective, first, is in China, how to resolve the challenges we're facing at home. And then, in the world there is the peaceful diplomacy, also called One Belt, One Road. So, One Belt, One Road is something linking China and all of the world: It's like our Confucian philosophers, and also like the Germans, with lots of famous philosophers coming from here, Schiller and so many! Those philosophers' thinking also needs to be connected together.

And then, in Africa: Africa is a wonderful continent, I think, unfortunately now still left behind. So from China and from the world, how should we work together to help the people in that continent? That's the main point.

Two Pictures of China

First, in China, the roadmap development goal—you all know on Oct. 18 in Beijing we had the 19th Party Congress, and all those very important documents will be released from the Party Congress. During the Party Congress, President Xi Jinping spelled out a long-term roadmap for the Chinese people, and the goal is to establish a moderately prosperous society, which we call the *Xiaokang* society. *Xiaokang* is a Mandarin Chinese word which means now moderate well-being. It's not so much a superpower yet, but just a moderate well-being society. So by counting, we should be out of poverty for all 1.4 billion population.

This is a tremendous job! Now we are entering into a new anti-poverty phase, called a "target anti-poverty phase." What is the meaning of "target"? About a half-year ago, I travelled to our poverty-stricken area in Shanxi province, and also I traveled to another, called Guizhou province, to see the poverty area, and I found that the local village heads will find out which households are still in poverty. So this is called the "targeting." And the heads of the village and the village leaders, their job is to help those poverty-stricken households to help them to get rich in a certain amount of time.

To bring out of poverty *all* of our 1.4 billion population by 2020, is not an easy job. The per-capita GDP

1. In China: Road Map and Development Goal to 2050

1) To establish a moderately prosperous society ("Xiao Kan" 小康社会）by 2020. Out of poverty for all 1.4 Billion population. Per Capita GDP reach $10000. (from $156 in 1978 to $8000 in 2016)

2) Two stages from 2020 to 2050:

  (1) To 2035, realize the Socialist modernization, Per Capita GDP reach $30000, GDP reach $43.6 trillion, become the level of middle developed countries;

  (2) From 2036 to 2050, become Prosperity, democracy, civilization, harmony and beauty Socialist modernization power

will reach $10,000. Now Chinese per-capita GDP is $8,000 in the year 2016; but back in 1978, our per-capita GDP was $156! So it was very, very poor, when this opening and reform was just starting. In Mao's time, we had a very interesting phrase, to express Chinese people's thinking about our three generations of leadership: The first generation of leadership, which is Chairman Mao—Chairman Mao helped the Chinese people "stand up," which means, before we were lying on the ground, being colonized, semi-colonized by Japan, but Mao helped the Chinese people stand up, but not to be well fed, not well clothed, just to stand up: political independence.

Then Deng Xiaoping's reform and opening up. Deng Xiaoping helped the Chinese people to eat well, now becoming rich, but only economically. But now, under Xi Jinping's leadership, so they not only stand up and eat well, becoming rich, but we should make more contribution to the world, becoming people who really enjoy life, and the country also enjoys dignity in the world. That's to establish a *Xiaokang* welfare society.

And then, how to reach that goal, the two stages from 2020 all the way to 2050. The first stage is to 2035, to realize the socialist modernization, per-capita GDP will reach $30,000; that's the goal. And then GDP as a whole will reach $43.6 trillion, becoming the level of what's called the middle-developed country. That's the first stage. And then, from 2036 to 2050 to become a country of prosperity, democracy, civilization, harmony—the beautiful socialist modernization power. That's the goal that's been set up in this 19th Party Congress.

So, when we think about China, there are two pictures of China, that is, generally speaking. If you go into details, there are a thousand different pictures of China. Those general two pictures—one is a rising power, seems very strong; this is the second biggest economy already, but—let me show the picture here—here is the general picture about China, this is the Global Economy by GDP. When we see the top right, United States of America, accounts for 24.32% of total global GDP; and then, to the left top, that's China, the yellow one—China accounts for 14.84% of global GDP. And then, a lot of others have double-digit percentages of GDP. So, in general, China is very powerful now.

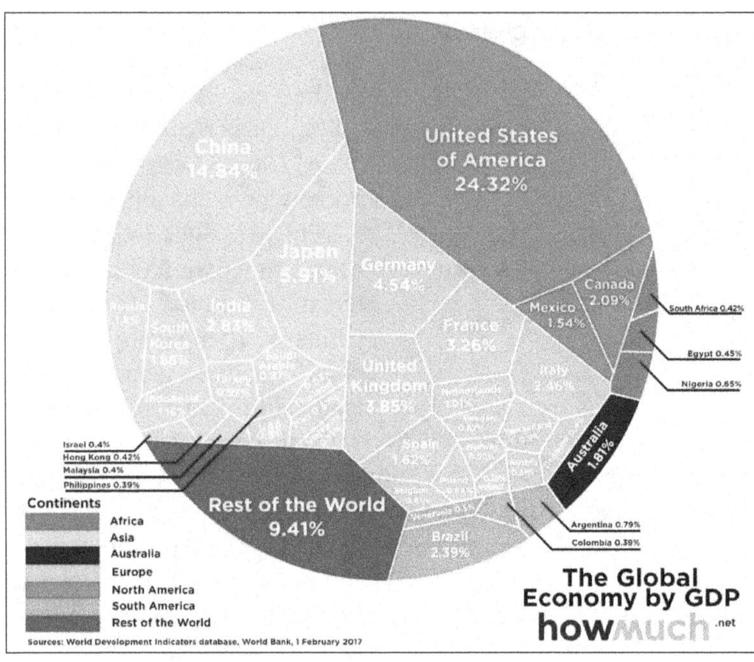

But, when we go to the per-capita GDP, this is the picture. We talked before about the *Xiaokang*. We're still struggling, heading forward toward *Xiaokang*, just to get to $10,000 per-capita GDP. Even recently,— let me share with you what the heated debate has been in recent days. Just a week ago in Beijing, there was a big fire; I think it was beyond the north Fifth Ring. That big fire cost around 28 lives. Eventually, after an investigation, we found that fire started in the basement, during the renovation of the building. And they found that there were a lot of people, migrant people living in that area, so fire safety measures hadn't been taken, and eventually the municipal government made a decision that all those places below the standard of fire safety have to be demolished. And then we had lots of debating from the rich saying, those migrant people, now they have to go back to their home towns. So that is the real picture.

It's another picture of China: Per-capita GDP is very low, and then the poor people, migrant people, are still struggling for their lives. In Beijing, winter season is very cold for those migrants. They have to leave Beijing and go back to their home towns with very short notice. That's another picture of China, so not saying that "everything's beautiful"; there are also very huge challenges.

So those two stages for 2050 are a huge challenge for China itself.

China Has Passed the Tests

So how to realize those beautiful goals? I think President Xi Jinping has done these things ever since 2013, when he took office. He has done things domestically, of course. Political development is to strengthen Chinese Communist Party, the ruling party's leadership, through the anti-corruption and anti-poverty campaigns. Anti-corruption is to do the things from the party leadership, but anti-poverty is to resolve the people on the ground, so there are two ends of those campaigns. But both ends of those campaigns are intertwined with each other. We started with anti-corruption, otherwise you cannot re-collect the confidence of the people on the ground to the ruling party. Although we started to resolve this poverty issue, you cannot claim it for yourself; you are still marching on the socialist path.

Anyhow, how to re-collect the confidence of the people and build the party's leadership? So three self-confidences have been put forward: those three, called the self-confidence, are the Development Road Confidence; the road we have chosen is called the socialist system with Chinese characteristics. So: Development Road Confidence, Theoretical Confidence, and Confidence in the State System—actually, the three things are the same thing, but have three different sides.

Maybe I should show the "shoe theory" President Xi Jinping mentioned, which means everybody wears our shoes, and the shoes should fit the feet, rather than the feet fitting the shoes. This is very simple knowledge, but when we deal with those very complicated theories, sometimes we lose sight of the simpler things.

So, we have this traditional story coming from this shoe theory. China has a 6,000 year history. Recently, U.S. President Trump mentioned this story: President Xi Jinping met President Trump and the First Lady to visit the gorgeous Forbidden City, the imperial palace, and he mentioned, China has 6,000 years of history, and President Trump answered, "Oh, yes, I know that! Egypt has a longer history—8,000 years." President Xi Jinping said, "Yes, yes, Egypt has 2,000 years longer history than China, yet both are very civilized."

So anyway, in our 6,000-year history, we have this phrase—when you learn Chinese, we have lots of beautiful phrases; all these phrases come from stories. This story mentions a guy who went to the market to buy shoes, but those shoes didn't fit his feet. Maybe the shoe style was beautiful, but it didn't fit his feet. And then, he immediately got out his knife, trying to cut his feet smaller, in order to fit into the shoes. This is the story: All our primary school students, they know this story when they write in Chinese writing; if you use a beautiful phrase you can get a higher credit, because you know the character very well.

So, it looks very simple, but it seems like our national condition is just like our feet: Our national condition, our character, our history, our population, our philosophy, all of that. Our feet cannot change, but those beautiful systems, liberal democracy, with some finger-pointing at China saying, "it's a one-party system," like you see a lack of transparency, and also maybe there's no fixed election—blah, blah, blah. We know what's better for China. At least those self-confidences are not naive belief! "I'm super, I'm super," but in fact, you just have very poor performance. That's not where self-confidence comes from. The self-confidence comes from your good performance.

What kind of things have we done that are good? Of course, from $156 per capita GDP, now becoming the second biggest economy, and also, we have gone through a lot of tests, such as the Arab Spring. When the Arab Spring took place in the year 2011 in Tunisia, there was lots of guessing, saying "China should be next," to have an Arab Spring very soon. Things were happening from Tiananmen Square, lots of reporters, every day they go to Tiananmen Square just to "catch the picture," to offer the picture to the newspaper and get it on the front page. But it's very disappointing: There is no such thing happening.

And then, there was a lot of

talk, after the 2008 financial crisis on Wall Street, with people saying "China will be next," and all those economic things about Deng. Before, they were even talking about China breaking up. But all of those tests, now the Chinese people and the government have gone through. Still, the economy is good; in politics people are united. And even the issue of terrorism, you see Egypt has suffered from another terrorist attack just yesterday. China also needs to watch closely for all those potential terrorists, maybe they are coming back from Syria, from Iraq. All of these are the great, great challenges.

Therefore, the confidence coming from those things—we have passed through all those tests, it's not just coming from empty things.

Also, put forward the Chinese Dream—I'll move a bit faster now—achieving the rejuvenation. I don't have the time to compare the Chinese Dream and the American Dream; there is a bit of difference from the American Dream.

Quality Matters

Secondly is combatting corruption. President Xi Jinping mentioned power must be caged by the system, and the rule of law must be strengthened. Also there are several channels to anti-corruption. The first is to improve the Party's conduct and strengthen Party discipline. Party discipline: Its power has been dramatically strengthened. A lot of tiger-level corrupted officials, and the mosquito-level corrupted officials—no matter whether you are tiger-level, like on the level of the Political Bureau, very high level those leaders; and the mosquito-level is the countryside, the village level, the

heads of villages. With all levels of corrupt officials, there is no method.

Now, also we have the Party school. I will not go into detail for lack of time. But one factor in the anti-corruption campaign,— I visited from time to time different provinces, and the people in the provinces, especially grassroots level people, now feel happy, because before, whenever you'd go to see a doctor, or you send your kids to school, you have to go through the back door; otherwise there's no chance for the poorer people, for their kids to get into a good school because corrupt behavior was everywhere, at all levels. But now, those people are saying, "Oh, thank President Xi Jinping, we no longer have these kinds of officials, bold enough to collect the 'red envelopes.' " In China, the red envelope is where you put the money to give to the doctor, so he will maybe be careful in doing the surgery for you; if he doesn't get the red envelope, you know, maybe he's not as careful in your surgery.

Now, those things are no longer there, especially among officials. And we also have the anti-poverty campaign.

Economically developed green economy and ecological progress. So, from "speed matters" now to "the quality matters." Before, in Deng Xiaoping's time, we had a slogan, "Only development matters: Development, development, development; GDP, GDP, GDP." All levels of officials, they just concentrated on how much GDP growth rate they achieved, otherwise there's no hope for their promotion. But now, GDP no longer matters: quality matters! So our environmental protection ministry is very powerful. They will go to different provinces to check on pollution. So if you are not concentrating on quality, you will not get your promotion anyway.

In Deng Xiaoping's time there was a very famous slogan—these are the words of Deng Xiaoping: "No matter whether it's a white cat or black cat, as long as it catches the mouse, it's a good cat." He was referring to the fact that no matter whether it's the capitalist way or socialist way, as long as it can make our GDP go forward, we'll take it. But now, people are saying "Black cat or white cat doesn't matter at all, we are far beyond that ideological thinking, but now it should be a Green cat." We cannot suffer from this pollution, and there's a lot of very bad air pollution.

One of our Party Congress documents talks about establishing the "beautiful China," so you can see a blue lake, a blue sky, very clean water, fresh air—those things we used to have before. But, after "development, development, development," you have money in your pocket, and you have to pay to put on your face mask [to protect against air pollution]. So, what's the meaning of life?

It just like a person, people were saying, before you reach 40 years old, you sacrifice your health to chase after money; but after you reach 40, you spend all the money you accumulated, trying to get your health back! That's the significance for China: Before we were sacrificing our sky, our blue sky, clean water, to chase after GDP. But now we have to use all the money in the GDP trying to get back the blue sky! That's the vicious circle.

How to pay attention to this quality issue in economic development? We made another change, which is a a production-driven economy to the innovation-driven economy. The pollution comes from what kind of thing? Coming from "Made in China"—China serving as the world factory, where everything was "made in China," so everything was spent in China, and pollution was left in China. So the world factory caused this pollution. We no longer want to be the world factory, we want to be the world's office, like India. The India President for instance said his country is a world office. We also want to be the world office.

Now, the world factory is also OK, but we need to improve, from those polluting ones, to becoming a very clean industrialization. So that is how to balance this growth and development, and inclusive development. Not to have only GDP growth rate with poor people and migrant people being chased away from the capital city. So, we have to be inclusive. All of these environmental developments, domestically speaking, this world of 2050, and internationally, are in the China One Belt, One Road initiative.

On One Belt, One Road, I don't think I need to go into detail, because when I entered this conference room, I saw lots of books over there [*The New Silk Road Becomes the World Land-Bridge*]—maybe I'll do some advertisement for those books—they are very rich for the world One Belt, One Road. So, I'll skip over that.

The Three 'No's'

Earlier, we were talking about the peaceful rising of China, and then because maybe some American friend said "it's very aggressive,"—"peaceful rising, it's very aggressive." And it's not so nice to the ear, so we changed the name to "peaceful development." So when our American friends put forward the Asia Pivot, we also thought it was quite aggressive, Asia Pivot. And so they also very nicely changed the name to the "Rebalancing Asia." So you see, we both changed and could meet in the middle.

So, from "peaceful rising" to "peaceful development," is the guideline for China's diplomacy, but some people have noticed, saying in Deng Xiaoping's time, Chinese policy seemed more or less to keep a low profile, and then in Xi Jinping's time, it seems more becoming active somehow, making more contributions to the world. Probably, yes, that's right. When you have the capacity, maybe you should make more contributions.

Let's skip over and go to the "Three No's," the three things we will not do: One "No" is "no intention to rely on so-called new colonialism." We have been labeled as the "new colonialists" in Africa, but not even our African friends have had the right to say whether China is the new colonialists or not. So I have no right to say that—our African friends have the right.

And secondly, the second "No," is no intention for military expansion, and war like Germany and Japan did in the Second World War.

And no intention to ask for the "China model" or to pursue ideological confrontation.

So those are the Three No's to explain why China's policy is peaceful development.

The Industrialization of Africa

Let's quickly go to the One Belt, One Road: This is just what I call—this is not official, it's what I call it—I think this is a 1.0 version of One Belt, One Road, because all those things you see, the Maritime one and the Silk Road continental one, go through 64 countries. In this 1.0 version, only Egypt is from Africa, among these 64 countries. But now, I think One Belt, One Road is entering 2.0 version—that is, now facing *all* the countries in the world. As President Xi Jinping mentioned to

Prof. He Wenping visiting Ethiopia's Oriental Industrial Zone

Shoe factory in Ethiopia (above and below)

the Latin American countries, "you are all welcome to join the Belt and Road." In the Chinese "40 Minutes," Xi said, all the African continent is now on the map of the One Belt, One Road, the whole African continent, especially after the May Belt and Road Summit in Beijing had taken place.

So now, its face is open to all the countries in the world, now it's inclusive. Any country that would like to join, I would like to say. You see, these are two leaders in the world: People are saying "America First" is the idea. You see from abroad, Trump in the White House saying, "America First." If anything is not too good for America, it's not good at all. But, for President Xi Jinping, the One Belt, One Road is to make the *world* better. It's not, "make China better," because with all this Belt and Road, the Chinese foreign exchange reserves, we're now enjoying the number-one highest foreign exchange reserves in the world.

So, we're going to use those foreign exchange reserves to build all those roads—connectivity! Connect China and other countries to join together, to build trade. And there are three connectivities we are talking about: First is the policy connectivity, China's One Belt, One Road initiative is relevant to countries, their own development strategy. For example, Ethiopia. Ethiopia has now been named as the "next China" on the African continent. It's not my invention, these words—many scholars have been published talking about which country in Africa is going to be the China in Africa, which means, developing faster! Faster and leading other countries forward. Most of them refer to Ethiopia.

Ethiopia has now reached an GDP growth rate, last year, as high as 8%, but the whole rest of the continent, especially the oil rich countries, are suffering from lower oil prices. So they have developed an industrialization strategy; their strategy and the China strategy should be connected. One is called the policy connectivity.

One is to make the world better, another is to make "America First," America better. So we look for the world, and America now looks for America only. That's the difference.

This is the connectivity—"policy coordination," our policy and the relevant country, not only in Africa, but policy connectivity first. And then, physical connectivity, to build infrastruc-

ture. Infrastructure to link the countries together. And then we push for trade, unimpeded trade. Allow me to share another number with you: In the world as a whole, there are 193 countries, but China serves as the number-one trade partner with as many as 128 countries! So, we are based on economic growth, based on export, based on trade. Now Chinese President Xi Jinping is holding high the flag of free trade.

So free trade and also inclusive globalization. When he joined the World Economic Forum in Davos, earlier this year, this is the first time a Chinese President had joined the World Economic Forum; before that, the highest official was only the Prime Minister. When he joined that forum, he put forward two things that China wants to push forward: One is free trade, and the other is the inclusive globalization.

That is the trade we want to push for as global trade,

British magazine is forced to recognize the changing face of Africa

and financial connectivity, financial integrity. China is pushing the One Belt, One Road to share its development with the world, and the way to push for such a major initiative was to establish what's called the AIIB, the Asian Infrastructure Investment Bank. This is a multilateral bank. And also the Chinese currency, the RMB, will also be widely used with those countries that are doing business with China.

And then, the people-to-people bond, that's another connectivity. So we're talking about five connectivities within this One Belt, One Road. People-to-people is very important. Before, China has been doing very well with the G2G, government-to-government, and then it has been doing very well with the B2B, business-to-business, but we have not been doing very well in P2P, people-to-people. Maybe Chinese people are very shy, so maybe that's one reason they're not very good at doing the P2P. So we should become more open and not so shy.

You know, in our education, like my son, all the way from primary school, kindergarten to the university, there's no debate in the classroom, you just take notes, take notes, about whatever the teacher is teaching. Take notes, take notes; no challenging, debating, raising questions. And we don't have political campaigns, so there are no such places for talking. There are lots of places for listening!

Anyhow, people-to-people contact, we need a lot of NGOs to go abroad.

Africa Is Rising

So very quickly, let's move to Africa. In Africa, we have commitment, that is the FOCAC, the full name is the Forum on China-Africa Cooperation. This forum

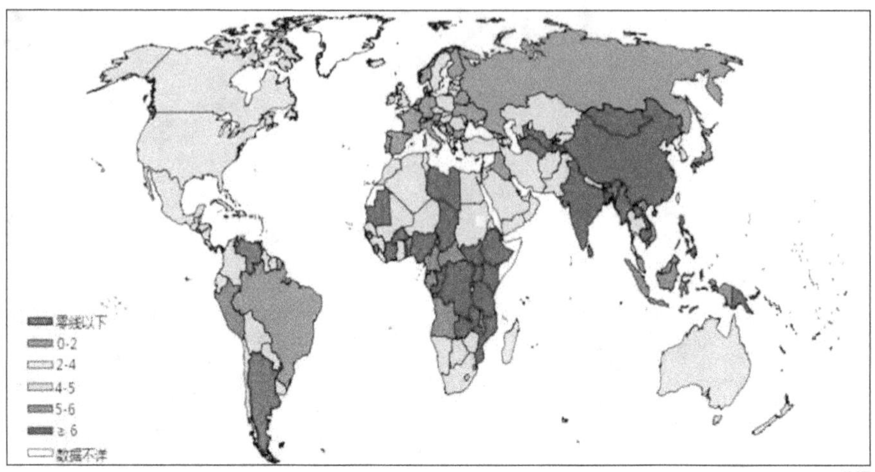

Deep blue shows areas of high economic growth in the past decade.

was established in 2000, and every three years there is a FOCAC meeting. The FOCAC meeting in 2015 took place in Johannesburg, South Africa. In that meeting, President Xi Jinping joined the meeting, put forward ten cooperation plans, and pledged the money—as high as $60 billion—to cover all ten areas: industrialization, agriculture, infrastructure, finance, environmental protection, and more.

The Belt and Road is very good for Africa's job creation. A lot of money has been earmarked to use for the industrialization of Africa. Let me just highlight in my last two minutes, the two areas, like two engines—like in an airplane, if you want to take off, you need two engines: One is industrialization, another is infrastructure. Without good infrastructure, there's no basis for industrialization—short of electricity, short of power, short of roads, and then it's very hard to make industry take off.

We have done a lot. Africa now is rising. Before, Africa was regarded as a hopeless continent, more than 15 years ago. But now, with kite flying over, now it's Africa's rising time. You see this map from the IMF, only in those deep blue places do they enjoy very high economic growth rates in the past decade—Asia, and Africa. So those two blue areas have above 6% GDP growth rates. They are mutually serving as the engines for each other—Asia's growth coming from Africa, Africa's growth coming from Asia. A booming future, industrialization creating jobs. I am sharing with you a lot of pictures of Ethiopia's Oriental Industrial Zone. I visited that zone—there is a shoe-making factory, lots of jobs have been created. You see, I visited that zone at least six times; every time I saw more business there.

Just to show you another infrastructure map: the Mombasa to Nairobi railway that was just finished at the end of May. We are going to build the second phase, from Nairobi all the way to Malaba in Uganda, and then that's an East African Community network. When this railway was finished—this is President Uhuru Kenyatta, saying this laid the foundation for industrialization. This shows people celebrating this railway connection, and this shows a man holding a paper saying "Comfortable, convenient, very soft, safe, and very beautiful." And here, very beautiful at 100 years old, a grandmother. [applause]

Thank you very much.

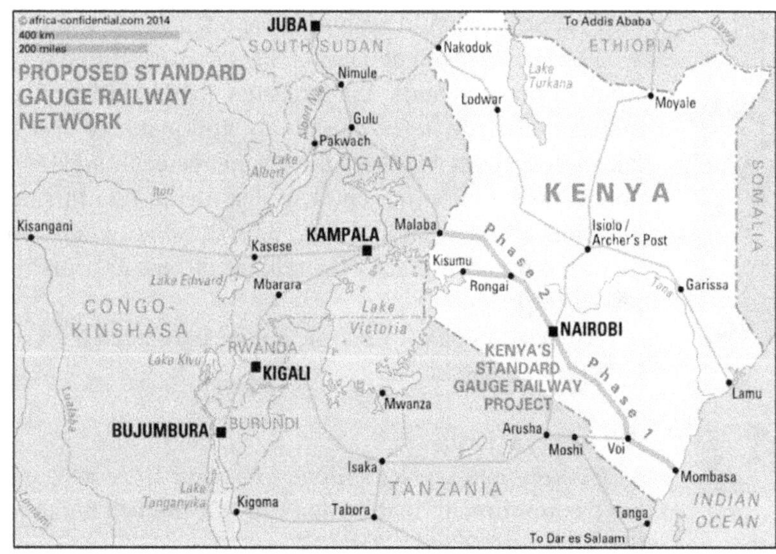

Map shows East Africa Community proposed rail network

DR. SAAD MOHAMMED MAHMOUD ELGIOSHY

Integration of Egypt's Transportation Plan 2030 with the New Silk Road Project

This is an edited transcript of a presentation by Dr. Saad Mohammed Mahmoud Elgioshy, former Transport Minister, Egypt, on Nov. 25, 2017, in Bad Soden/Taunus, Germany. Subtitles have been added.

Good Morning! I am Saad Eligioshy, a Ph.D. Doctor, a specialist in transportation, airports, and roads. I am the former Minister of Transport in Egypt (2015-16).

I'd like to thank Mrs. Helga Zepp-LaRouche for her nice invitation. Also I'll thank the organizer of this conference, the Schiller Institute, which really touches on some of the benefits for Egypt. The lecture I heard from you today was very interesting.

In my presentation I will speak about Egypt, a very old country—7,000 years—and how it will interact with the New Silk Road. You heard, before me, a very nice presentation by Prof. He Wenping, about the New Silk Road, how it will work in Africa. As I said, I represent one country in the north of Africa. I will speak about how we can interact with the New Silk Road.

I will focus on the integration of Egypt's transportation development plans. I'll discuss the transportation issue, which is an infrastructure issue, which affects the development of *any* country. So, transportation development plans and the New Silk Road Project.

In a very brief introduction, I'll discuss the current transportation system in

Dr. Saad Mohammed Mahmoud Elgioshy

Egypt: its existing hierarchy, challenges, and opportunities, and how we can interact.

Then I'll discuss the Egyptian Transportation Development Plan 2030—how an African country thinks about development; and also speak about the New Silk Road Development Corridor close to Egypt, Africa, the Middle East, and how we can integrate with this giant project, especially in the transportation sector, in Egypt.

The transportation sector in Egypt serves an area of 1 million km² and a population of 100 million by the end of this year.

Egypt has a road network consisting of about 30,000 km of rural highways, and 60,000 km of urban roadways, with about 1,800 bridges. We have a network of three subways lines in the capital, with a total length of 100 km, and are building another three lines.

Maritime transport. Realize Egypt is a costal country situated between two main seas, the Red Sea and the Mediterranean. We have 15 commercial sea ports.

I am speaking, just for a moment, about land water. We have about 3,000 km of land water river ways, with more than 43 land ports in Egypt.

1. **Introduction (Egypt Transportations System).**
   (Existing Hierarchy, Challenges, Opportunities)

2. **Egyptian Transportation Development Plan 2030.**

3. **Silk Road Development Corridor in Egypt, Africa, and Middle East Area.**

4. **Integration Areas between Egypt Transportation Plans and Silk Road Plans.**

Speaking briefly about the Egyptian Transportation Plan 2030 and its main features: Our vision is to increase the capability of the transportation sector to fund its plan to achieve its goals; to obtain a greater share in the volume of international and regional transportation; and to maximize and optimize the use of

cc/Abdelrhman 1990

Present day international coastal road near Alexandria, Egypt.

science and technology, and research and techniques in management.

We're supposed to provide high quality transportation for persons and goods, securely and safely, at the lowest cost, while supporting national social economic development. Also we're supposed to secure national security requirements.

We have big challenges to overcome to accomplish all this: An ascending increase in population with an annual growth equal to 1.85%; defects in the transportation service, which do not match and are inappropriate for the people; the mutual increase in freight from 1.51-2.32 million tons; the increasing annual growth in land transport which affects the road network; the absence of private sector—and this is a very important point—partnership in infrastructure projects; the absence of a multi-modal transport system; the lack of technology applications and logistical services; and the lack of trained and skilled labor. We have an increasing number of transportation accidents, due to these factors.

We have a very old railway system. It is the second oldest in the world, after the United Kingdom. It was built in the 18th Century, with an extent of about 9600 km, and it serves about 540,000 pax [secure electronic payment terminal], with about 1,100 daily trips. I am speaking here about facilities and capabilities. You see the numbers: 750 stations, 3,100 passenger coaches, 11,000 freight cars, 808 locomotives, so and so.

If you go to the land water sector, [it's] the same, as I mentioned before. We have 3,500 km of river lines, 43 active ports, and 15 controlling gates. We have seven dry land ports and seven logistic areas.

Looking at all of this, which I skimmed over quickly, I am speaking about opportunities. Does Egypt have opportunities in the transportation sector for the whole world to come and invest with us? Yes, we have! We have a lot! We have a lot of opportunities in Egypt for roads and bridges. We have already have about 8,500

- **<u>Roads & bridges projects</u>**

- **New construction and upgrading of existing roads 8500 km.**
- **New construction for main arterial axis over the Nile river (sum of 12 axe including bridges).**
- **Construction of New bridges in the national road network (sum of 21 bridge).**

km of new construction underway, as well as upgrading of existing roads. We have new construction of additional main arterial accesses over the Nile River, including twelve new bridges. I'm speaking about the 2030 Plan. And also construction of twelve bridges in the national road network, for a total of 21 new bridges, over the next 12 years.

The railway sector is also full of opportunities. A lot of companies from all over the world are asking to bid on these projects over the next 12 years. I'm speaking about supplying 600 passenger coaches (2nd class air-conditioned); 110 power unit coaches; upgrading and modernizing 300 locomotives; supplying 50 new locomotives (3,000 hp), supplying six complete trains, upgrading 2,700 cargo coaches, and supplying 1,530 new cargo coaches. You can read with me. Most of these investment opportunities are virgin, and need some kind of sharing by investors from all over the world: upgrading three main workshops (locomotive overall, locomotive renovation and maintenance); supplying two complete sets for railway maintenance; supplying four machines for railway compaction; upgrading and modernization of safety and control systems, including completion of 3,000 km of an electric signaling system, equipping 600 locomotives with ETCS-L (the European Train Control System—a central signaling and control component for the all-electric signaling system); construction of 500 km of new lines and upgrading 750 km of existing lines; construction of 1,200 km of high-speed service; and construction of nine cargo stations.

Then there's also upgrading of the railway system itself. Upgrading the signaling system of cargo railways—many projects.

The land water sector is full of opportunities too. I am speaking about upgrading two navigation roads, Cairo-Aswan (1,200 km) and Cairo-Damietta (200 km), and the construction of five new land water ports and upgrading four existing ones. I'm speaking about upgrading six dry ports and construction three new ones. I am speaking about more than 50 billion Egyptian pounds.

As for tunnels and metro (subway) service, we already have three main subway lines (Cairo Metro), each of them 40-50 km in our capital city. We're looking to upgrade all of them. We want to upgrade the tram lines in Alexandria and in Cairo, and construct three new lines for Cairo. We have had many offers, starting from last year, to study the plans and to partner with us for these projects.

The maritime sector is a big sector, and full of investment opportunities. I am speaking here about the ports of Suez and Ras adabia in the north of Egypt, and the ports of Sfaga and Sharm El shikh in the south. All these ports have very nice opportunities to build cruise and container ship terminals.

That is what we have in Egypt.

Now, I would like for you to concentrate with me on the next part of my presentation, about what the New Silk Road brings to Egypt. To easily reach to the interaction between the two points, we can see that the New Silk Road, from its concept—and my colleagues will speak more about it—offers the possibility to overcome geopolitics once and for all. The Belt and Road Initiative, as my colleague mentioned, is based on the "win-win" concept.

I'd like to concentrate on the phrase "win-win concept," because I'll use it again. Cooperation among all nations of the world. All the individual nations should pursue the development of their own national transport networks, but adjust them to adapt to the continental networks, to benefit from them, to contribute to their quick implementation and development, and to avoid duplication of efforts. That's also very important.

The New Silk Road has a new financial system, composed of three main entities: the Asian Infrastructure Investment Bank (AIIB), the New Development Bank, the New Silk Road Fund, and the Contingency Reserve Arrangement. All that is exclusively designed to fund investment in the real economy, with the goal to awaken justified optimism, in particular in developing countries, to defeat poverty and underdevelopment in the near future, as mentioned before.

We have now reached the goal of this lecture: how the New Silk Road Project is touching Egypt in the transportation sector.

As planned, there will be a 56,500 km Trans-African Highway (TAH), the main routes being Cairo, Egypt to Dakar, Senegal (8,600 km); and Cairo, Egypt to Cape Town, South Africa (10,200 km). Now, that's a highway!

As for rail, we find there are two giant lines. One of them is the African Integrated High-Speed Rail Network (AIHSRN), which will connect all the capitals of Africa to-

cc/Wrightbus

Egypt National Railroad (ENR) diesel locomotive passing through El-Giza station, Egypt.

- **New construction and upgrading of railway line:**

  *** new construction of 500 km New lines.**

  *** upgrading of 750 km.**

- **Construction 350 New cargo railways.**

- **New high speed train 1200 km.**

- **New construction for 9 cargo stations.**

• **Tunnels and Metro**

- **Upgrading current lines (line 1&2).**

- **Completion phase 3&4 for line 3.**

- **Upgrading of tram line in Alexandria.**

- **Upgrading of tram line in Cairo.**

- **New construction for line 4 - greater Cairo.**

- **New construction for line 5 greater Cairo.**

- **New construction for line 6 greater Cairo.**

Present day African highway landscape.

gether with a high-speed railway network (HSR). There is a plan to form a group for "Sino-Africa cooperation in railway and high-speed railway." Financial institutions, railway construction companies, and railway operation management companies can work on that.

Inland water very important. As I mentioned, Egypt's population today of over 100 million lives on a narrow strip of land on the banks of the Nile River and Delta, about 5% of the land. More than 95% of the land is vacant. Africa Pass will open the desert in the west of the country for development and habitation. We hope so. The project will also revolutionize the economies of the North African sub-Saharan nations.

For the Congo River Basin there is the Africa Pass program. I think it will be a good project. Flowing from the tributaries of the Congo River, Africa Pass envisions a 3,800 km long canal, paralleling the Nile to the east, reaching to the Qattara Depression in northwestern Egypt, opening millions of acres of land to be cultivated. This area will become a breadbasket, not only for the rest of Egypt, but also for other countries.

Construction of the Jonglei Canal would be a good sign for cooperation and for doing something for the connectivity of inland water between the South and North.

Integration between the Egyptian Transportation Development Plan 2030 and the New Silk Road Project, from my point of view, could consist of Egypt completing its National Road Network (MINTS 2010), now in Phase 3 of construction, which will add 5,000 km, and integration with the New Silk Road Project's planned routes, which I mentioned earlier: Cairo-Dakar (8,600 km) and Cairo-Cape Town (10,200 km). If we did that, it would be a good job!

Egypt is right now implementing a lot of upgrades to its National Road Network, mainly the Cairo-Aswan road, and the Cairo-Alexandria road. The NRN could be integrated with the AIHSRN and with the "Sino-Africa" program.

We are looking at Egypt's upgrading of its main land water route Alexandria-Aswan, and working with the Nile Basin countries which are currently studying a route to connect Lake Victoria with the Mediterranean, to integrate that and the Congo Pass program and the Jonglei Canal (both mentioned earlier) with the New Silk Road. Egypt looks favorably upon all these projects.

I'd like to say something very important. We in Egypt from 1952 experienced many kinds of cooperation for development of our country. We can't forget history. If you forget history, you will do nothing. We started in 1952 with many disciplines. We went to the communists in the Soviet Union; then we went to America—capitalism. We went to many, many countries seeking their help in development. Finally we went into the Arab Spring. What happened? We didn't accomplish anything; we didn't get any-

New financial system

 Asian Infrastructure Investment Bank.

New Development Bank, the New Silk Road Fund and the

Contingency Reserve Arrangement.

▪exclusively designed to fund investments in the real economy.

▪Awakened justified optimism, in particular in developing

countries.

▪Poverty and underdevelopment can be defeated in the near future.

▪Offers the possibility to overcome geopolitics once and for all.

▪"Belt and Road Initiative" is based on the idea of "win" win

cooperation among all sovereign nations of the world.

▪the individual nations should pursue the development of their own

national transport networks projects, but adjust them to adapt to

the continental net-works, to benefit from them, to contribute to

their quick implementation and development, and to avoid

duplication of efforts.

thing, because, as my friend said, "Their feet don't match our shoes." All the time.

Egypt, as I said at the beginning, is a very old country. It has its own culture, its own understandings. The problem is how to match any country, any model, any development model with our culture. That is the problem; that is the real problem. That is the real challenge.

If this prestigious institute desires to propose development plans to Egypt, I suggest you plan a workshop in Cairo to allocate interaction areas, present the possibilities of interaction, and discuss how to enable such interaction. Don't expect us to interact in all areas; we are supposed to interact with *our* plan. Remember, Egypt already has a plan. If China with their giant New Silk Road Project comes to Egypt, they must first study our plan, and then determine the areas in which they can locate their cooperation with the countries of Africa, before they can be accepted and not considered a new colonial power coming to Africa. The people are afraid of that, as she said. That is a very important point. We can avoid that through workshops in Cairo, Senegal, Nigeria—all the countries which lie in the route of the New Silk Road.

Exchanging plans between the New Silk Road Project stakeholders and the Egyptian Ministry of Transport, for example—I'm speaking about transportation infrastructure—is very important. When I was Minister of Transport, I was visited many times from representatives of China. We had many discussions. But nobody asked me about *our* plans. Nobody asked me about *our* plans for development of transportation in Egypt and how *their* plans could be integrated with ours. They asked all the time about *individual* projects, and these projects never fit in our shoes, as did our feet.

I'd like my colleagues and my friends in China to understand this point, and to exchange plans between the New Silk Road plan and the Egyptian plans. After that we can analyze the methodology of plan integration—how we can interact with each other, how we can work with each other to discover the methodological basis for such cooperation. This is very important. After that, we can easily implement recommendations for cooperative construction.

Again, the New Silk Road plan is a very giant plan. It is a very smooth and very friendly plan. We need to cooperate with the whole world—with China, with Europe, with America, with any country which matches our plans, which matches our dream. Egypt has a mankind dream, and needs to fulfill it by its culture and by its way.

Thanks a lot! Thank you very much! [applause]

A Future for Europe after the Euro

Helga Zepp-LaRouche: We will have now one more speaker, Mr. Zanni from the European Parliament from Italy, and then we will have a video message after that, and then we will take some time for discussion.

Rep. Marco Zanni: Thank you again to the Schiller Institute for this invitation and for having organized, once again, such a very interesting conference. The speeches of the people that spoke before me confirms that there is a worldwide com-

Rep. Marco Zanni

munit, not just in Europe, in Africa, and in China, that is thinking about a better future for our people in the world.

Today I will talk about the future of Europe, because it's clear that something is not functioning well in this continent, and it's clear that what is happening is not only at a political level. We are meeting in Germany, and the debate about a future government of this country is the sign that something is going wrong. But also, we must also consider the situation that

Xinhua/Marios Lolos

Greek pensioners protest in Athens, Greece, on Oct. 6, 2017 against the planned new round of cuts to their income under the third Greek bailout program.

we are living in at a microeconomic level, and the fact that the European Union is not able to address and to solve the three main challenges and problems that European citizens are living through today. The first one, the most debated, is clearly the economic and financial crisis that is still alive in our continent; the second is the problem of internal security and all the problems related to terrorism; and the third one is the problem related to the management of migration flows, that are affecting a lot of countries, and especially my country, Italy, because of our geographical position as the bridge of the European continent and in the Mediterranean area.

It's pretty clear that we have to challenge the rhetoric, that there is no alternative to the European Union, with which the European establishment has campaigned in the last twenty years, that the European Union is a political infrastructure that should remain, and continue in the future. This super-state, this institutional framework for Europe is not able to solve problems, is not able to create better conditions for Europeans, and is not able to fulfill the promises that European politicians made, especially after the end of the Cold War at the end of the 1980s.

So it's time, today, for a new European political class to think about what could be an alternative project for Europe that could challenge the actual framework of the European Union. As I said, we are challenging— and I, personally, as a representative of the European and Italian people in the European Parliament—are trying to challenge this TINA (There Is No Alternative)

rhetoric. Because we need an alternative institutional framework for the European people.

Let me clarify one very important thing: The European elites are trying to use the term "European Union" term as something that is close, or is comparable to Europe. I would like to stress the fact that in my opinion, the European Union and Europe are two very different concepts. Europe is a geographical, historical concept that includes a lot of countries. The European Union is a political infrastructure, a political framework, that was founded in 1957, so it's here, but it has been present only for a short time period, compared to the history of Europe, and it includes only twenty-eight countries—a huge part of the countries in Europe—but they are not the totality of the countries and people living today in Europe.

Today, as I say, the European Union is not only failing in addressing problems of the people on this continent, but the policies and the political framework of the European Union are also making these problems worse. The policies and rules that we are applying and which were built into the European Union in the last twenty years, are creating divergencies and asymmetries, not only between countries, between the countries participating in the Union and in the Eurozone, but also between people inside the same country. Germany is one of the best examples of what is happening at the country level with this European Union framework.

The poor people, or let's say, the majority of people, are negatively affected by the rules agreed to at the European Union level, and the elite are strengthening their powers to shape European legislation to protect their interests. This situation is causing suffering not only in the so-called PIGS, the Southern European countries of Portugal, Italy, Greece, and Spain, but as I said, also in the core European countries, such as Germany, the Netherlands, and the Scandinavian countries. And the political situation of those countries is the proof of this situation.

The Failure of the EU

In the last election German voters decided not to support the more traditional parties, the Social Democrats and the Christian Democrats of Mrs. Merkel; they decided to support so-called populist, euro-skeptic par-

Homeless person in Hamburg, Germany.

ties, right-wing and left-wing parties. The strong support that the AfD (*Alternativ für Deutschland*) and also the liberals, the FDP (Free Democratic Party) received in the last German election is also a sign that, people and voters of the country that received the biggest benefits from European rules and the Eurozone framework, now are challenging the future of this project, because this project, the Eurozone and the European Union rules, are negatively affecting their lives. The economic situation of people living in the former East Germany is really bad. Unemployment is very high, people are living on money transfers from the central state and richer regions, and the situation is very bad. It is comparable to the situation in other member-states, such as Italy.

In Italy, we are still coping with a lot of problems in terms of youth unemployment. The youth unemployment rate in Italy is close to 40%, an unacceptable rate. Total unemployment is stabilizing, but only at close to 11-12%, another unacceptable level. A macroeconomic labor market indicator that the ECB is using to assess the situation in the labor market of the Eurozone countries shows that the rate in Italy is the highest in the European Union. It's close to 30%; that means that we have 40% of our working population under stress. And the policies of the European Union and the Eurozone are not only not addressing this problem, but are instead strengthening differences and asymmetries inside the countries.

Another problem that we are facing is the problem related to our financial system and to our banking system. There is a huge debate inside the European Union, as to what should be the future of our financial institutions. After the big financial crisis in 2008 and after the sovereign crisis that affected the Eurozone in 2010, the European institutions decided to set up a very comprehensive set of new rules, trying to regulate the banking industry in the Eurozone. This huge amount of rules, this new framework, was called the Banking Union. This was based on three pillars: The first one is common supervision of the biggest financial institutions in the European Union; the second pillar is the Single Resolution Mechanism, the so-called bail-in rule. This is a unique mechanism at the European level that would intervene to resolve banking crises should one of those big institutions get into trouble; and the third pillar, which is not agreed upon— we are working on it—is the common deposit insurance for all the Banking Union countries.

It's clear that this new framework is not functioning well. The biggest mistake of this framework was to try to create regulations that would cope with the consequences of a financial and banking crisis without doing anything to try to set up instruments and tools to avoid the *causes* of a financial crisis. This new framework of rules created more instability in the financial sector inside the Eurozone, because now, not only taxpayers, as happened in the past, have to, so to speak, participate in the bail-out of a big financial institution, but also savers and common people who invested their savings in financial products—in bank bonds, in deposits, or in other very simple financial instruments—have also had to participate in the bail-in of bank institutions. The European politicians, in 2012, when the Banking Union was agreed to, promised that with the Banking Union, no more would taxpayers' money would be used to save big financial institutions. What happened in reality? We now have three years of experience with more than 10 banks that have been "resolved" according to the new Banking Union framework. What happened was that not only did taxpayers have to participate in the resolution of banks, but also common people and savers who were misled with financial products, had to participate in this.

In Italy, in 2017, we had two very big financial problems related to our banking system. One was the suddenly famous resolution and saving of the *Banca de Monte dei Paschi di Siena*, which was one of the world's first banks, founded at the end of the 15th Century and operating in Italy and all over Europe since that time. The other one was the resolution of two regional banks, which were very important, because they were located in one of the most industrialized and developed regions of Italy, Veneto. I'm referring to the resolution of *Banca Popolare di Vicenza* and *Veneto Bank*, two Venetian banks that were resolved in April 2017.

The cost of the resolution of these two banks was very high. More than EU20 billion of taxpayers' money have been used to save these two banks, and more than EU15 billion in shareholders' value, in bondholders' value, have been used to save these banks. It's clear that this framework cannot be efficient in making our financial system more resilient, more effective in supporting the real economy, more effective in supporting public infrastructure investment, more supportive in assuring strong support for European citizens in pursuing their entrepreneurial activities, and so on.

An Alternative is Required

It's clear that we need a different framework.

The big question that we are working on, and that is very important for the future of Europe, is this: Is the European Union the best institutional framework that we can create or that we can have in Europe, in order to address these very important problems that European citizens are facing today? Looking at what happened in the last twenty years. According to my experience in the European institution in the last four years, my reply would be: "No. Clearly, no."

Why? Because the European Union today, and the rules that we agreed to at the European Union level, are impeding member states and governments in addressing properly the problems that European people are subjected to.

What can we do to challenge the European Union's "There Is No Alternative" rhetoric, that European institutions and European leaders are using today to justify their failure and to go on with this failing project? We have to create a new institutional framework that will start from the core of the European democracy, that is, member states. We have to give back to member states powers in order to shape the right mix of policies to cope with the crisis today. That means, give back to member states the power to set up their monetary poli-cies; the power to set up the right mix of fiscal policies that they want. It's clear that a "one size fits all" approach cannot work, and is not working! A single monetary policy for 19 different countries that are facing 19 different economic cycles cannot work! Today, Germany probably would need a less accommodative monetary policy; Germany would need to have interest rates rising; Germany will need the end of quantitative easing. But it's clear that Italy and other countries need the continuation and increase of competitivity and more of an accommodative monetary policy.

The fact that we agreed—and I'm going to conclude with this point—that we agreed on a public balanced budget rule, is impeding European countries and governments from dedicating appropriate resources for infrastructure investment, and that is not happening only in Italy, but also in Germany. Public investments in infrastructure in Germany are a bit low! They are not recovering after the financial crisis.

So, it is clear that we have to create a new framework of rules in Europe, in order to challenge this European Union framework that is failing to address European countries' policies. We have to create another Europe that will be the bridge between the Asian countries, the developing countries, the new world powers that are approaching the elite, and the United States. That's a role that Europe can do, but with the EU's current policy, with these provocations that the European Union is bringing face-to-face with Russia, with this new Common Defense Project provocatively putting of a lot of military forces at the border with Russia, the future of Europe and the European countries will be really, really tough.

We have to regain our sovereignty. We have to return power to member states, not only in terms of fiscal policy and monetary policy, but also in terms of diplomacy; and we have to coordinate all European sovereign countries in order to create more positive political scenarios for Europe, and for our historical partners outside Europe—Russia, Turkey, Iran, China, African countries, Egypt, and a lot of developing countries. It will be very important to create and set up a cooperative "win-win" approach that could benefit not only the Italians, not only Europeans, but people worldwide, in order to ease conditions, and to create development and opportunities for people in the continent of Africa, in order to stop these migration flows that are affecting the European Union.

Thank you very much for your time.

European Petition to President Trump To Implement Glass-Steagall

Liliana Gorini: My name is Liliana Gorini. I'm the chairwoman of *Movisol*, LaRouche's organization in Italy, and a close collaborator of Mrs. Helga Zepp-La-Rouche and Mr. LaRouche for the last forty years. I say this, because I haven't been at conferences for physical reasons, and now I've finally made it: So many people may not know me.

I wanted to commend what Zanni just said about the situation in Europe, and particularly my country, Italy, and confirm fully what he said about the effects of this crazy policy of the European Union on the population, and in particular, about the bail-in. There are already victims in Italy of this bail-in policy and the Banking Union: Two pensioners took their lives because they lost all their savings. These were not rich people. These were normal people who had saved money throughout their lives, which was simply stolen with the bail-in. It is not a solution; it is actually creating more problems.

After the problem with the Veneto banks, we now also have one of the main cooperative banks in Genoa, *Carige*, which is going broke, and people are scared. They not only are losing jobs, and the economy appears to continue, only because of people living on

their savings. Italians tend to save money, but if they also lose their savings they will not only not have a job, but they will also not be able to survive. So the Greek nightmare is becoming very, very close for all Italians.

But, in the Spirit of the New Silk Road, there is a solution, so I want to bring the good news to everybody in the spirit of optimism which Mrs. LaRouche gave in her opening speech: We in Italy have been having a discussion which we started many years ago, based on the Four Laws of LaRouche, and particularly on the first one, on Glass-Steagall. The debate created by Movisol—by us—has now brought eight bills for Glass-Steagall into the Italian parliament; in the meantime, it is being debated in four regional councils. Recently, there was a discussion in the Finance Committee on this.

Last month, we decided, because the European Union forbids the discussion, to bring the discussion from Italy to the United States. In what way? We wrote a letter to President Trump, to remind him about the promise he made during the election campaign, to reinstate Glass-Steagall. One hundred-thirty members of parliament signed it—of the Italian Parliament, the European Parliament, including Mr. Zanni, who collected eight signatures from members of parliament for this letter, and state legislators: regional councilmen from Lombardy, Veneto, and people from Southern Italy.

Many other people signed this: Important economists, journalists, leaders of newspapers, myself—I was also among the first signers, of course.

Our idea is to bring this letter to Congress in January, in order to move the bipartisan bills forward which have been proposed in the U.S. Congress. As you know, a few Republicans and many Democrats introduced [or co-sponsored] bills. Glass-Steagall was in the party platforms of both the Republican and the Democratic Party, as it is in the party platform of most Italian parties. We in Italy will have national elections, probably in May. All of the banking separation and Glass-Steagall [proposals] are in the party platforms of all these parties in Italy, from left to right.

This is thanks to our campaign in Italy. In particular, I want to introduce you to this young man – who is the reason why I am here, because he drove me – Massimo Coldamassaron [ph]. He's the one who collected the signatures, going to politicians and beating them over the head, saying, "I want to save the future of my children, and you have to enact Glass-Steagall, otherwise, we will be without a country very soon." He has this collection of petitions, and he asked—and I'm doing this, since we're here—if there are any of you, like for sure, Hussein Askary, Ulf Sandmark, Jacques Cheminade, whoever has a position, some kind of prominent political role, we would like to add names to these 130 Italians, a few people from France, from Germany, from Sweden, from Denmark, so that when we go to Washington, it will be clear that not only Italy, but all of Europe, all of Europe wants LaRouche's Four Laws and Glass-Steagall.

So, please come to me or to Massimo, and we will add your signature, and we will make sure that this petition ends up in the hands of President Trump: We will make sure. Thank you.

[applause]

Zepp-LaRouche: I want to fully endorse this idea. I think that's a very useful proposal, so anybody from any country who wants to support this initiative should really contact Liliana and Massimo. I think the Europeans have not gotten their voice together, and I think what Representative Zanni expressed, that there *is* this discrepancy between the policy of the European Union and the ability of the European nations to defend their own interests, is very clear. I think that this conference can be a very good starting point to escalate such a demand.

I would urge all of you, go to Liliana and help this campaign, not just by giving a signature, but by making a commitment to do what Massimo did. All of us can go to the politicians, to mayors, to parliamentarians, and demand that they defend the common good.

Just to reinforce what was said on the financial crisis: We are sitting on a complete powder keg. The signs that the crisis of 2008 is repeating itself on a much larger scale are overwhelming. The debt crisis is bigger than in 2008; all the parameters—the derivatives, the indebtedness of states, of corporations, student debt, the real estate crisis—all the parameters are about 40-80% worse than in 2008. And the European Union has just issued a guideline that they have no tools, other than stealing the money of the citizens. This is really a very dangerous moment which we should use as a starting point to go into a real mobilization, to get these Four Laws implemented.

The Need for Europe to Cooperate with China in the Industrialization of Africa and the Middle East

HUSSEIN ASKARY

Extending the New Silk Road To West Asia and Africa

Hussein Askary is the Southwest Asia Coordinator of the Schiller Institute and is based in Stockholm, Sweden. This is an edited transcript of his address to the International Schiller Institute conference on "Fulfilling the Dream of Mankind," Nov. 25, 2017, in Bad Soden/Taunus, Germany, which he presented under the title, "Extending the New Silk Road to West Asia and Africa: A Vision of an Economic Renaissance." Subtitles have been added.

Hussein Askary

This report, with the same title as my presentation, which I co-authored with my colleague in the Schiller Institute, Jason Ross, was inspired by the ideas of Lyndon La-Rouche and the incredible fight launched by Helga Zepp-LaRouche, the Schiller Institute, and the LaRouche movement worldwide over the past 25 years to make the dream of the New Silk Road a reality.

There is nothing unrealistic about what I am presenting here about Southwest Asia and Africa. The reason I am optimistic is that the new paradigm in international relations has taken hold, and the old imperial order is fading away. The other, more subjective reason for being optimistic is that we will continue fighting to make this happen.

The empire is still dangerously lurking, like a wounded tiger, and it might attack at any moment. However, the ideology of the empire and its axioms and beliefs about the relationship be-

tween man and nature, between man and man, and between nation and nation, will continue to be a source of danger to the human race. For example, the belief that money makes things happen. Or, the environmentalist idea that human activities to develop and raise the living standards of society always negatively affect nature and the environment, and that humans should, simply, be prevented from growing in numbers and in standards of living.

But through China's constructive interventions, this is being pushed back, as we describe in detail in out report.

One very important point, which must be emphasized, always, is that neither I, nor the Schiller Institute, or for that matter China, is intending to impose on, or dictate policies to the African nations. What we are offering is friendly advice, lessons that other nations have learned the hard way, and of course certain universal scientific, cultural, and moral principles that apply to all human societies. African nations, and each one of them as an independent and sovereign nation, have to choose to join this development of their own will.

Now, Southwest Asia or West Asia, and Africa have been associated with wars, mass emigrations, famine, and epidemics. But this is about to change as the winds of the New Silk Road blow into the sails of the new paradigm, which is led by the BRICS nations, and China specifically.

In January 2016, Chinese President Xi Jinping visited three of Southwest Asia's major countries—Egypt, Saudi Arabia, and Iran. Saudi Arabia and Iran were deeply involved on different sides of the war in Syria. One week before that visit, the Chinese Foreign Ministry issued the first ever China-Arab World Policy Paper, in which China's contribution to the region is defined by extending the New Silk Road to this region and cooperating with these nations on large scale transport infrastructure projects, nuclear power, fighting desertification, and so on. China is offering the rest of the developing world all of its experience in development and poverty reduction. This is the first time a major power has opened its entire technological tool kit to other nations.

The Potential of the Region

Southwest Asia and the Horn of Africa, combined, has unique characteristics. This fantastic geographical location between Asia, Africa, and Europe has two-thirds of the world's petroleum reserves, nearly $2 trillion in

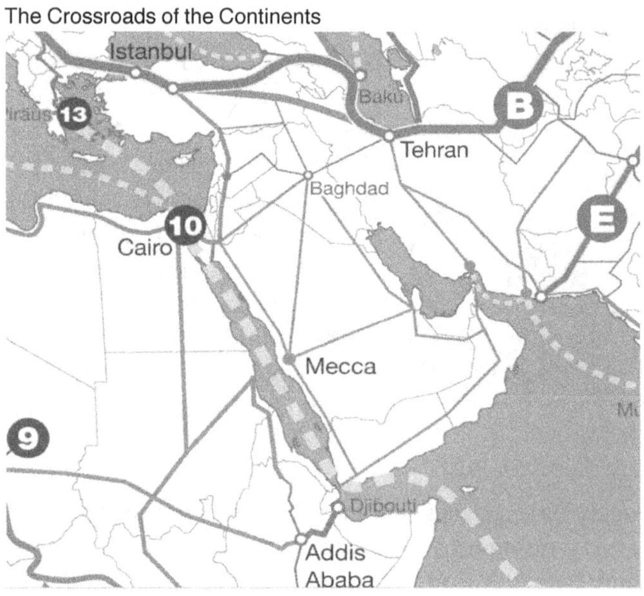
The Crossroads of the Continents

foreign currency reserves in the sovereign wealth funds of the Gulf states, and most importantly, about 400 million people, most of them below the age of 30. This region is very hungry for technology and investments in infrastructure, including transport, power, water, telecommunications. This is, in other words, potentially one of the greatest markets for capital goods on earth.

The governments of the region, themselves, realize now the importance of cooperation with the East to build their physical economies. Nations that are coming out of destructive wars, such as Syria and Iraq, and others that are still waiting to do so—Yemen and Afghanistan—will require enormous technological and logistical input to rebuild themselves.

Egypt, which is a natural bridge between the Mediterranean and the Indian Ocean, between Asia and Africa, is already positioning itself, to take the lead in this process, with the expansion of the Suez Canal and establishment of new industrial zones, and investing in transforming its transport networks to adapt them to the Belt and Road Initiative.

Through Egypt and the Maritime Silk Road, we arrive in Africa.

The African nations have had many real developmental plans since independence, such as the *Lagos Plan of Action* of 1980, which includes large-scale infrastructure projects to connect all countries, such as the Trans-African Highway. But none of these projects have seen the light of the day. The reasons are many, but they all point in the direction of the old paradigm of geopolitics, in which one nation or one tribe is pitted against the other, in order to take riches out of Africa and give nothing back except weapons, so that the guerrilla groups continue to protect the gold, diamond, and cobalt mines, and the oil fields. The typical attitude in Europe and the United States towards Africa is negative: Africa represents famine, poverty, epidemics, civil wars, dictatorship, and on and on. However, China's attitude is that resolving all of these problems is a great opportunity, because the remedy exists and it has been applied in China itself, with incredible results.

China and the Industrialization of Africa

China in Africa now, according to a report issued earlier this year by McKinsey Consulting, is the No. 1 trade partner, the No. 1 infrastructure builder, the No. 1 in growth of foreign direct investment, the third in aid, and so forth.

The Trans-African Highway Network (TAH)

This is the result of many years of a consistent Chinese policy, of technology transfer, win-win cooperation. Referring to China's experience, President Xi Jinping said, at the December 2015 Summit of the Forum on China-Africa Cooperation (FOCAC) held in Johannesburg, South Africa, "Industrialization is an inevitable path to a country's economic success. Within a short span of several decades, China has accomplished what took developed countries hundreds of years to accomplish and put in place a complete industrial system with an enormous production capacity." Encouraging African leaders to pursue a path of industrialization, a call never heard from leaders of industrial nations in the West since the assassination of President John Kennedy, President Xi stated: "It is entirely possible for Africa, as the world's most promising region in terms of development potential, to bring into play its advantages and achieve great success.... The achievement of inclusive and sustainable development in Africa hinges on industrialization, which holds the key to creating jobs, eradicating poverty, and improving people's living standards."

To give you a clear picture of the two different attitudes, I would like to present some data here:

China is not the No. 1 investor in Africa! No! It is No. 1 in the rate of increase of investment. It is the United States and Britain who are number one and two. However, take a look at what and where they are invest-

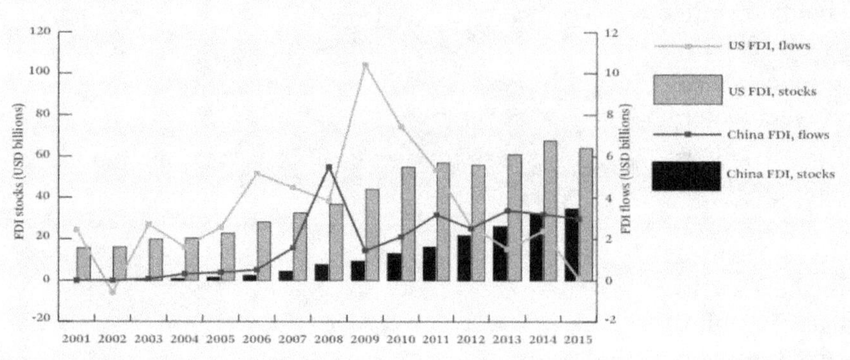

Chinese and U.S. FDI to Africa 2001-2015

ing in comparison with China.

Of course, China's positive involvement in Africa provoked a massive campaign of lies in Western media and think tanks, a large-scale brainwashing campaign based on lies which has affected many people's attitude towards China, even among many Africans. I take one specific case study, a study of land-grabbing, because it makes people in Europe and the United States so emotional. Taking agricultural land from hungry Africans?

A Case Study

I am sure that every one of you has heard in some form or the other that China is moving millions of workers and farmers to Africa to grow food for Chinese markets. It looked like this in 2009, in the midst of a terrible global food crisis: "A million Chinese farmers have joined the rush to Africa, according to one estimate, underlining concerns that an unchecked 'land grab' not seen since the 19th century is under way." This is from an article in the British **Guardian**.

A million Chinese farmers have joined the rush to Africa, according to one estimate, underlining concerns that an unchecked 'land grab' not seen since the

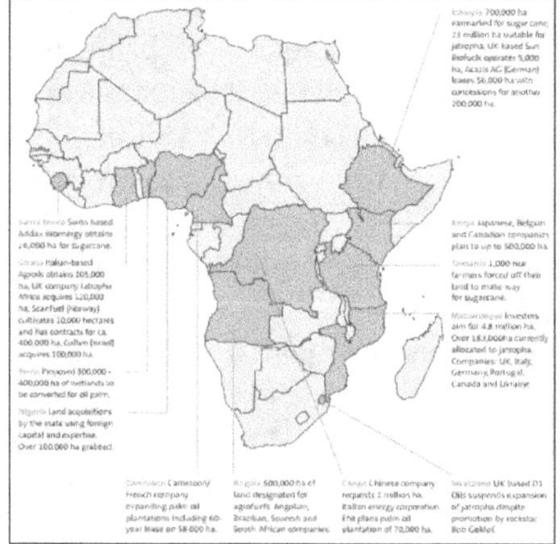

Friends of Earth Europe, 2010: "Africa: Up for grabs—The scale and impact of land grabbing for agrofuels"

What is outrageous about this article is that the so-called "estimates" the *Guardian* refers to, are supposed to be in a report issued by the International Fund for Agricultural Development and the UN Food and Agriculture Organization. So I read it. It mentions **nothing** about "a million Chinese farmers," (!) and to the contrary, it asserts: "However, as yet, there are no known examples of Chinese land acquisitions in Africa in excess of 50,000 hectares where deals have been concluded and projects implemented. China's 'Friendship Farms' in various African countries are formally owned by a Chinese parastatal organization, but are mostly medium scale, usually below 1,000 hectares."

What we discovered from investigating this matter of land-grabbing, is that not China, but European companies, mostly British and Scandinavian, have been involved in grabbing large swaths of fertile and water-rich land in Africa to produce what? Food? No. They plant sugar cane and jatropha to produce ethanol and biodiesel for cars in Europe.

Investigations by the EU Parliament, investigative reporters, and environmental organizations such as Friends of Earth prove this point. Not only must the attitude towards Africa change, but the very prevalent way of looking at economic development must also change. As we pointed out in the speech of President Xi in the Johannesburg meeting of FOCAC, the new definition of sustainable development is industrialization.

Consistent with that new definition, mega-projects are back! And they are not built to glorify dictators, but to transform whole economies, nations, and even whole continents.

As my colleague Jason Ross put it: "Africa must leap ahead, not crawl slowly forward!" U.S. and European politicians have been proposing that developing nations should not "make the mistake" of rapid industrial development, and instead must crawl slowly, through appropriate technologies. Appropriate for Africans, why? Why not other technologies used in the United States and Europe, such as nu-

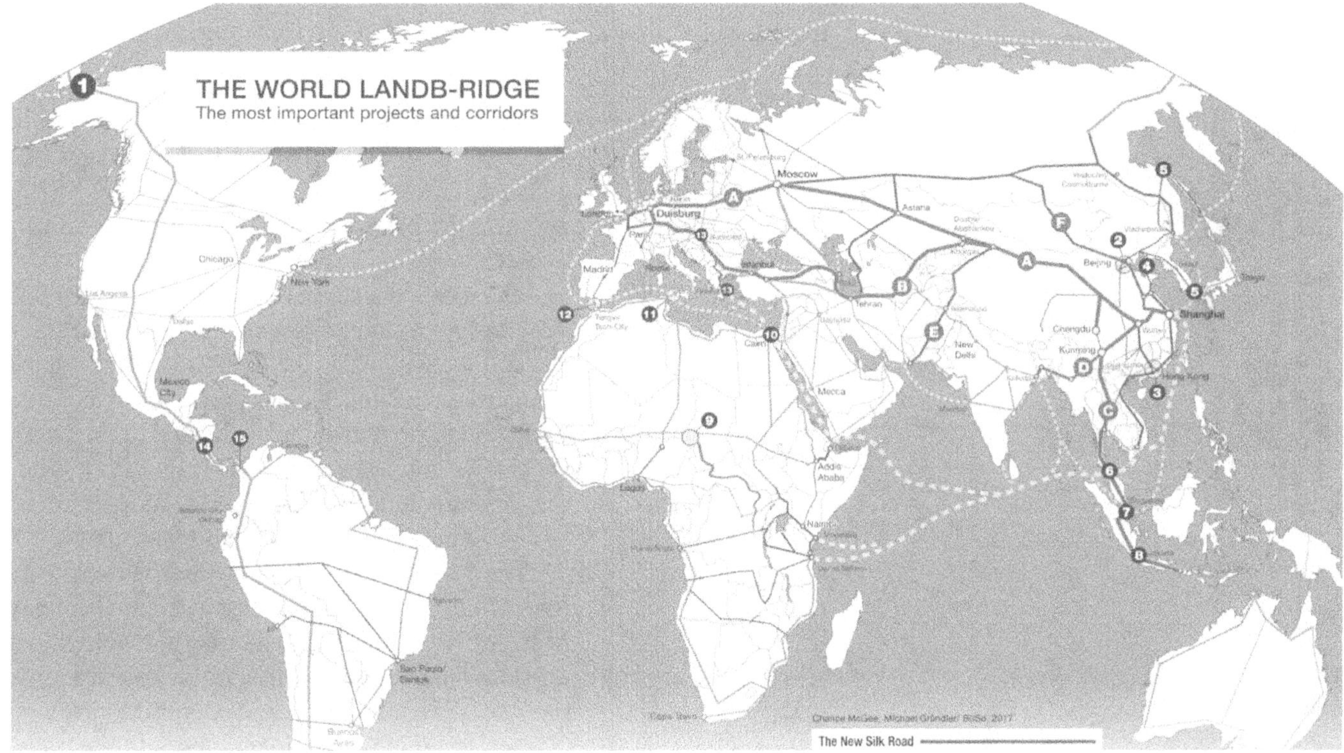

clear power? Why should Africans have a different kind of technology? What do you mean by appropriate?

No! The irony of the case of the development of Africa is that the deficit of basic infrastructure in Africa, as was the case in China, is an advantage, in that it allows nations to skip the intermediate stages of development that occurred over centuries in the industrialized countries, to leapfrog directly into the technologies that are at the frontier. This is the approach that China has taken, deploying high-speed rail and magnetically levitated trains, and fourth-generation nuclear fission technology, leaping ahead of the stagnating United States and Western Europe.

Recommendations

Our recommendations for the Southwest Asia region and Africa are:

• Establish a regional infrastructure development bank, similar to the Asian Infrastructure Investment Bank (AIIB). Simultaneously, each nation should have a national credit mechanism, a national development bank, to internally finance part of the infrastructure projects.

• Integrate the infrastructure networks through state-of-the-art, high-speed railway systems; build an integrated navigation system across the rivers and lakes of Africa; develop the full potential of the hydropower of the rivers; build fourth-generation nuclear power plants for power generation and desalination of seawater; and focus on the upper end of the value chains of the mining industry through petrochemical and metal industries, rather than relying on export of raw materials for income.

• Create a new "green revolution" in agriculture, similar to the Indian and Asian green revolutions, through developing new strains of higher yielding, disease- and drought-resistant crops. Reduce post-harvest wastage of agricultural products through better processing, preserving, and transporting of agricultural products.

• Focus on science and future-driven educational programs, with special focus on producing scientists, engineers, and a work force capable of handling frontier technologies such as nuclear, high-speed transport, and even space technologies.

Finally, a quick review of what mega-projects are underway in Africa, and what is still to be done.

Let's look at development corridors. When we look at the New Silk Road or any other routes, we are not thinking simply in terms of trade—transporting an item from point A to point B. We regard these as *development corridors* that carry technology, materials, and manpower to open whole regions for physical economic development, including along the routes them-

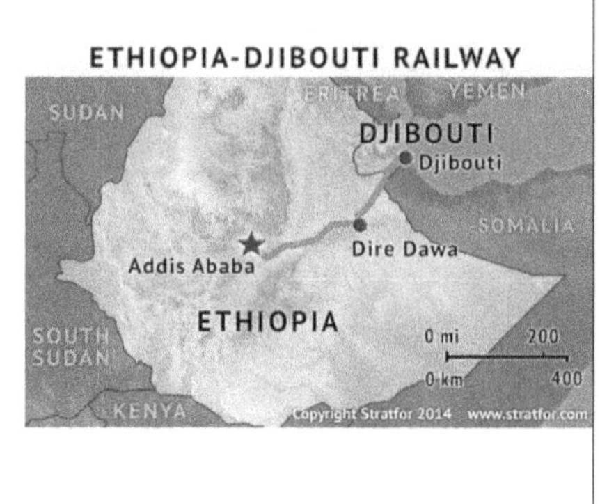

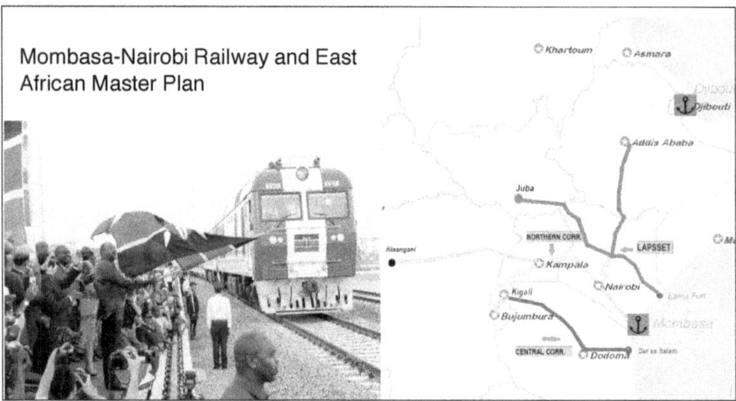
Mombasa-Nairobi Railway and East African Master Plan

Morocco: High-Speed Railway (TGV) 2018

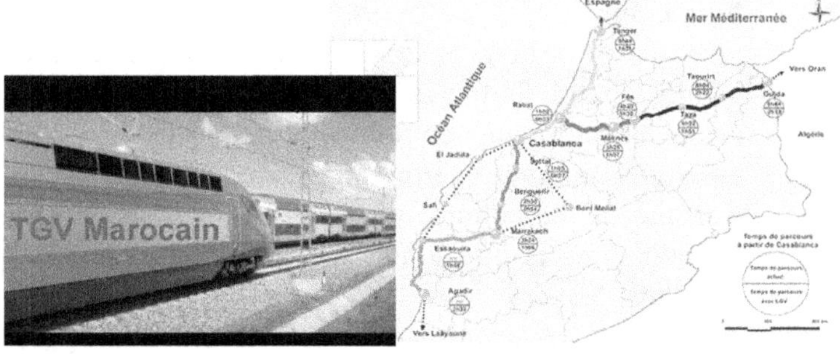

Angola-Tanzania: Benguela and TAZARA Railways

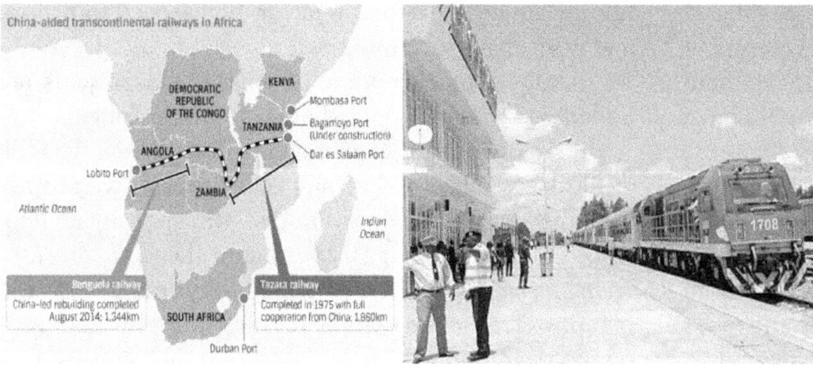

selves.

We will use this map from the African Union's Highway Network as a reference point, which is also the basis for the new standard gauge rail routes that China is building in Africa, and also the basis for the new High Speed Railway Network.

The most spectacular projects completed this year were the standard gauge railways in Ethiopia and Kenya. First, the Djibouti-Addis Ababa standard gauge line. This is part of the Ethiopian national rail plan to connect all parts of the country and neighboring countries. Ethiopia is building several industrial zones too, as part of its five-year national development plans.

The other railway is the Mombasa-Nairobi line. This is part of the East African Railway Master Plan. There are three major development corridors under construction in East Africa now: the LAMU, Northern, and Central corridors. These corridors will be integrated into the transcontinental corridors in Central and West Africa.

Another landmark achievement was China's rebuilding in 2015 of the 1,344 km Benguela railway in Angola, practically taking away the British Empire and its old colonial tracks, replacing them with new standard gauge tracks.

In West Africa, several rail projects are underway along the Atlantic Coast of Nigeria, and to connect Lagos to Nigeria's larger inland cities.

The first high-speed railway on the continent, in Morocco, is nearing completion. It is being built in cooperation with French companies.

We propose that the following mega-projects are of highest priority:

- Transaqua
- The African Integrated High-Speed Railway Network
- A trans-African river navigation system
- The Grand Inga Dam
- South Africa's High Temperature Nuclear Reactor Program
- The Gibraltar connection
- The Italy-Tunisia connection.

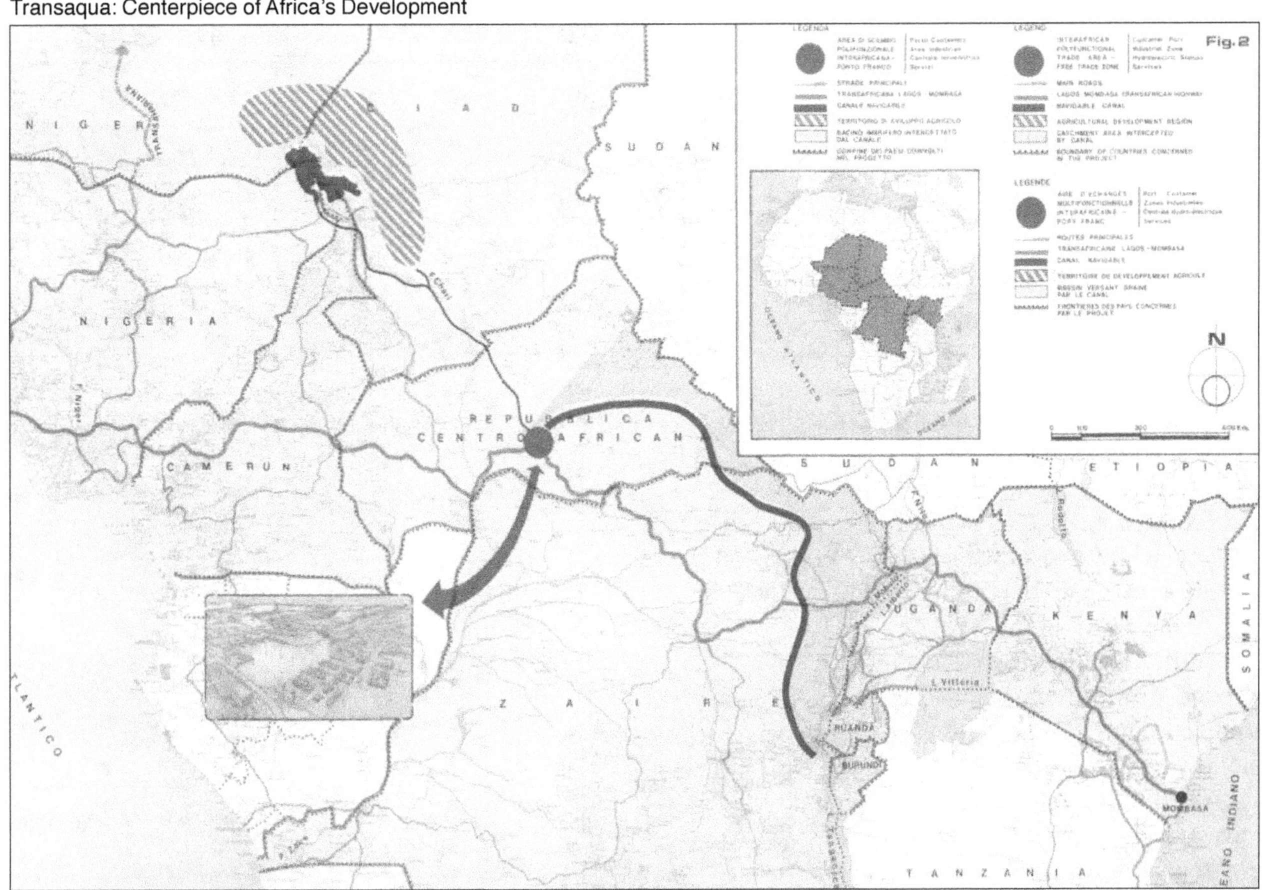

Trans-African High-Speed Rail Network

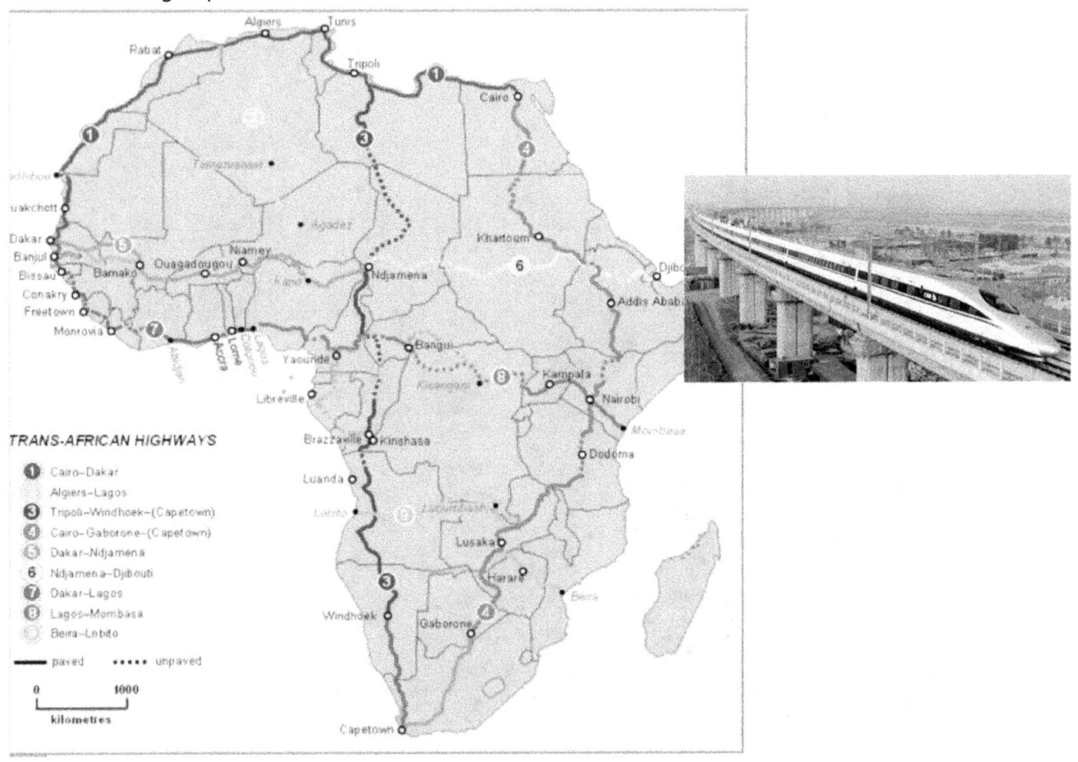

Conclusion

According to the UN, by 2050, the bulk of the world's population growth will take place in Africa. Of the additional 2.4 billion people projected to be born between 2015 and 2050, 1.3 billion will be added in Africa. By 2030, Southwest Asia and Africa will have jointly contributed the greatest population growth (46.9% above 2015 levels) of all world regions, reaching 1.9 billion in 2030, with an amazing median age of only 23 years. Those who think this is a major problem belong to the old paradigm, while those who believe this is a great opportunity, belong to the new.

If we get things to work, we might see Africa evolve into the next decade into "a new Chinese miracle with African characteristics." As Mr. Lyndon LaRouche has always emphasized: It is the future that determines the present, not the other way around. It is our vision of the future that defines our actions in the present. Thank you!

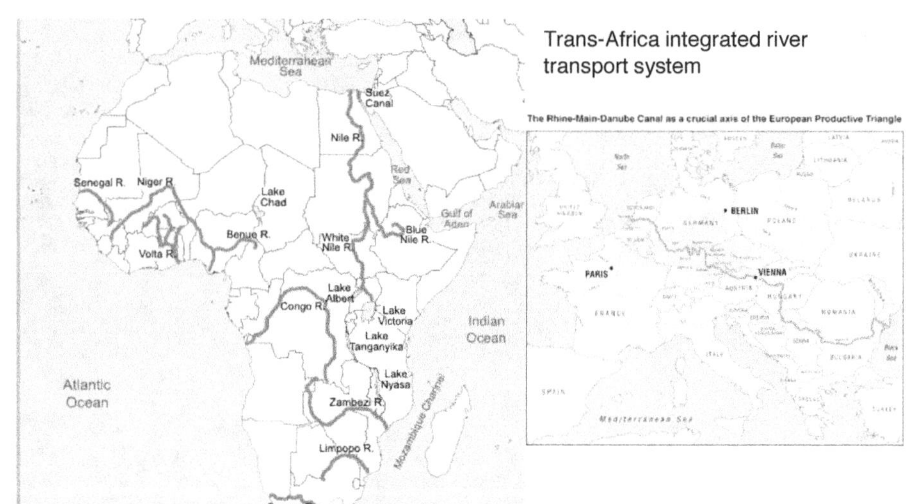

Trans-Africa integrated river transport system

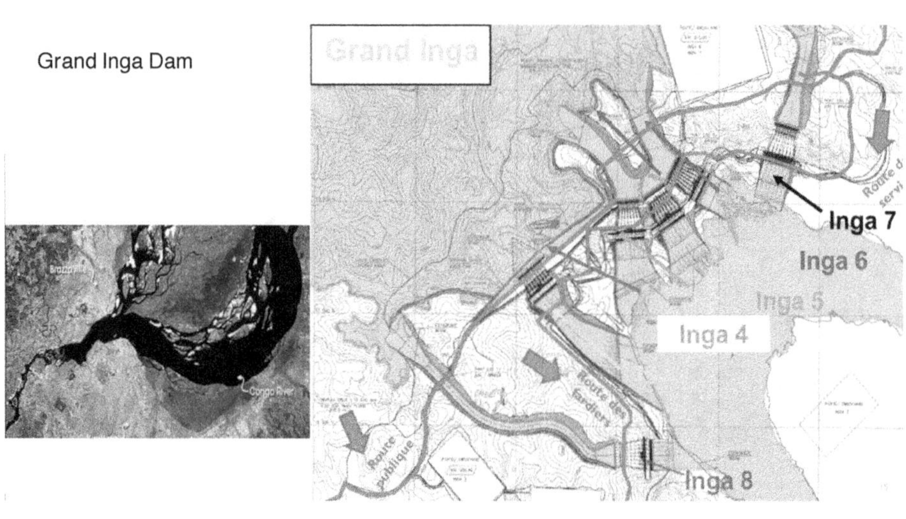

Grand Inga Dam

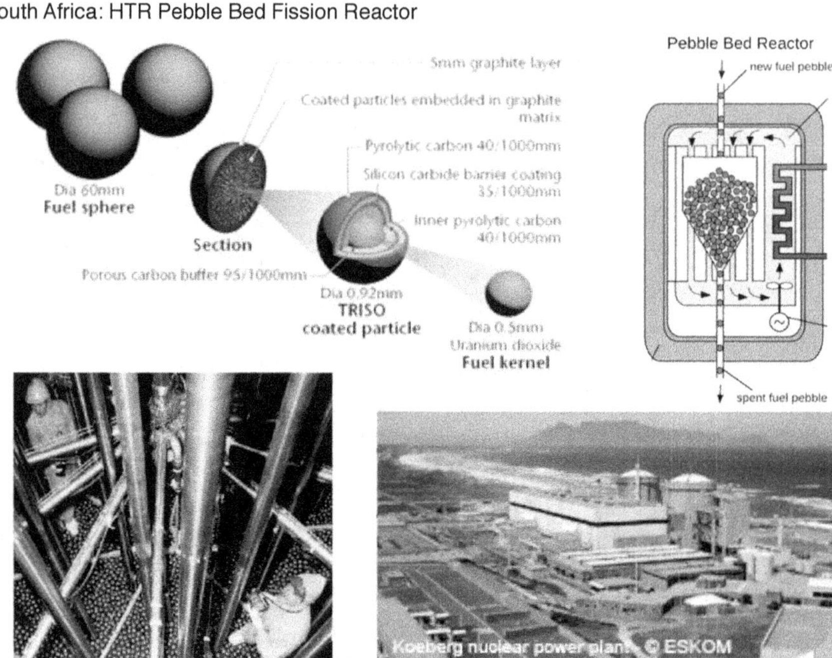

South Africa: HTR Pebble Bed Fission Reactor

FRANCO PERSIO BOCCHETTO

Italy-China Alliance for Transaqua

This is an edited transcript of a presentation by Franco Persio Bocchetto describing the Transaqua project to the Nov. 25-26 Schiller Institute Conference.

HUSSEIN ASKARY: Our next speaker is from Italy, Mr. Franco Persio Boccetto, Foreign Director for Bonifica, S.p.A., Italy.

FRANCO PERSIO BOC-CHETTO: Good afternoon to everybody, and to Ladies and Gentleman. I'm very glad to be here at this very interesting conference. I was really amazed listening this morning, especially to the speeches of Schiller Institute President Helga Zepp-LaRouche, and the one of the enthusiastic Professor He Wenping. And also I was interested in hearing the speech of Professor Askary, who introduced the Transaqua project that I would like to show and present here.

The Transaqua Project

The Transaqua project is perfectly in line with the vision of this conference, which is "To Fulfill the Dream of Mankind." Transaqua, as maybe you know, was conceived more or less about 30 years ago, by our firm Bonifica. Perhaps at that time, it was too innovative; maybe in that time nobody was really interested in developing Africa. But nowadays conditions are really different and maybe this is the time to revive the project: Maybe we can call it "Transaqua 2.0" in order to start the development of this great dream for Africa.

Maybe most people think Transaqua is only a problem of transferring

Franco Persio Bocchetto

water from the Congo Basin to Lake Chad, but this is not the vision of Transaqua. First of all, everything starts from the problems that are related to Lake Chad. We are going to show you the actual situation of Lake Chad.

Lake Chad was one of the largest endorheic lakes in the world, and maybe the largest in Africa. The lake is situated in the Sahel region, at the crossing of the borders of four countries: Niger, Chad, Nigeria, and Cameroon. The total catchment area of Lake Chad is very huge: 2,434,000 sq km. Eight countries, including Algeria, Cameroon, Central African Republic, Chad, Libya, Niger, Nigeria, and Sudan are using the water resources from Lake Chad. The main inflows of Lake Chad are from the Chari River, and Chari and Longone River, and the main outflows are evaporation and infiltration. For this reason, it's an endorheic lake, because it does not drain to the sea.

The Chari River and Longone River flow from south to north, and this is the actual Lake Chad. The lake basin has a very unstable equilibrium as there is no surplus water flowing to the sea. The only outflows are infiltration and evaporation. If water is used upstream, the lake cannot but shrink.

Lake Chad always had great oscillations, due to natural climatic fluctuations. Now, especially in this period of climate change, we must follow very closely what will be the future of Lake Chad. Lake Chad is suffering from the increase in population and subsequent water consumption, mainly for irrigation, and in addition, the decrease

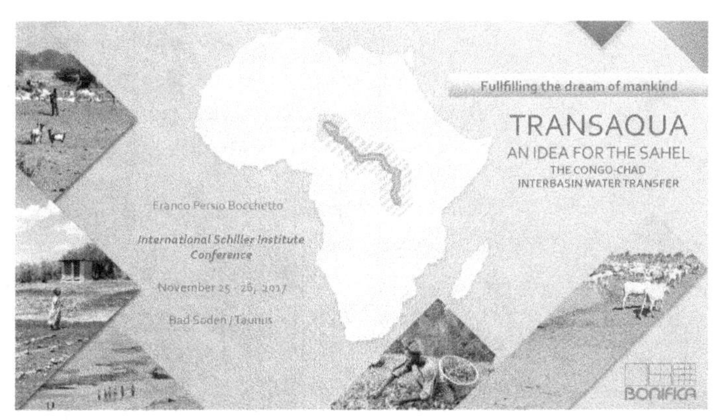

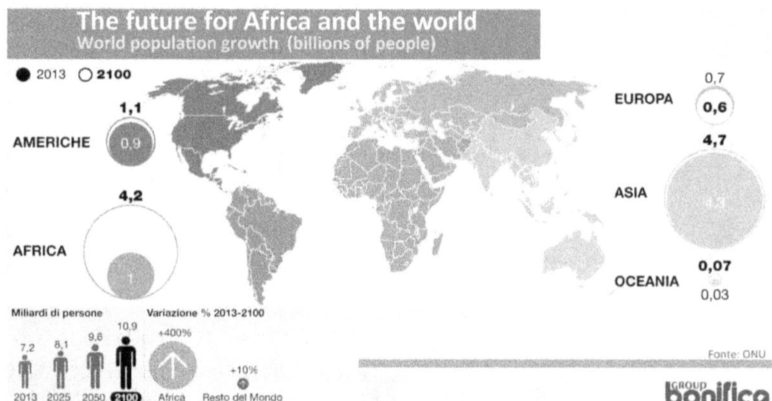

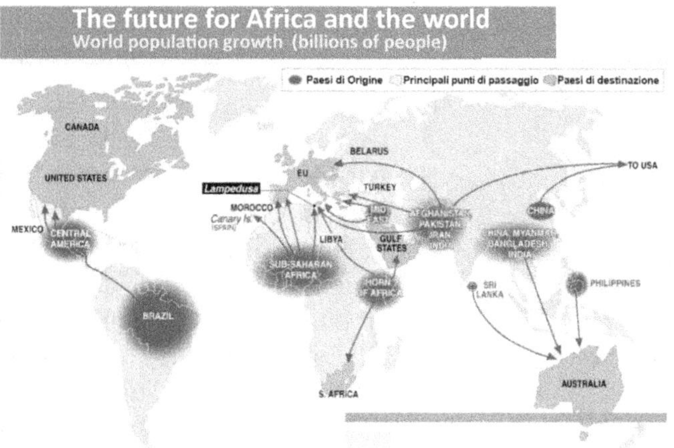

of rainfall. Lake Chad's surface in 1973 was more or less 25,000 sq. km. As you see, in 2015, it decreased to 2,500 sq. km, while the population within the basin has grown from 8 million to 30 million people, more or less.

As a consequence of this drought and drying up of the lake, agriculture development increases pollution, ecological destruction, and extinction of rare species. The economy of the surrounding countries and region is severely threatened by reduction of the lake's surface levels and volumes. Average food production and household purchasing power have been continuously reduced since the 1980s. Humanitarian, ecological, and economic crises are developing rapidly as the volume and surface of Lake Chad are drastically reduced at an alarming and accelerated pace.

Also, it's important to show the evidence that in this region, the consequences of this are also all the problems related to Boko Haram, which is really active in this region due to the poverty of this region.

How to mitigate the Lake Chad drought: Well, thinking of the problems of Lake Chad, we have to think about the future. And the future in 30 to 50 years will be very, very dramatic for Africa in a certain way. As you see, it is forecast that real growth of the population, between today and the year 2200, will grow by 400%. So the problem is, what will happen when, within 30-40 years you will have the doubling of the population in Africa, and also in those Sahel regions.

We heard today in the earlier speeches, about the New Deal and the optimistic vision of Chinese President Xi Jinping, and we really hope that, due to the positive strength of China, they will really succeed in helping the world help to develop, and that these regions will have help from the Chinese for development. There are a lot of projects that are going on as Mr. Askary has showed us in the context for all of Africa. But, it is important, also to set up and improve the Transaqua project in Central Africa, in the middle of Africa, the part which is poorest and where the desert is continuing to make inroads.

The consequence of not doing this is a huge migration into the rich countries, and of course, Italy and Europe are suffering from these consequences. Most of the people come from the Sahel region, so I think that Europe has to help to improve the Transaqua project, in order to develop all these countries, and bring food, agriculture, and fisheries as a way to eliminate poverty in this region.

Over the years, the Lake Chad Basin Commission, created by the states around Lake Chad has really done great work in facing up to the shrinking of the lake, and for the realization of

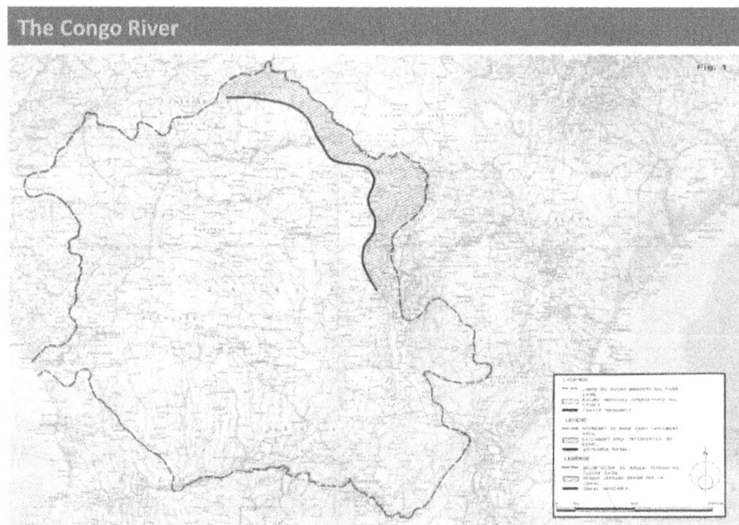

The Congo River

numerous national and transnational projects, to optimize the use of water resources and mitigate possible disputes between the states.

What to do next? What will the next challenges be for the Lake Chad Basin Commission? First of all, in the medium term, there are projects that are going on to mitigate the Lake Chad drought, of course, projects that tend to sustain the existence of people, improve the efficiency of water use, through new research, innovative organization, based on the use of smart technologies to improve the efficiency of system coordination and control. First of all, a very big monitoring system should be set up in order to control the consequences of climate change, control all the problems related to agricultural use, and control the consequences of national and transnational projects that are being done in this region.

We can be very optimistic, but due to the growth of the population, the long-term measures cannot be other than to think how to transfer large volumes of water from the Congo River Basin to Lake Chad.

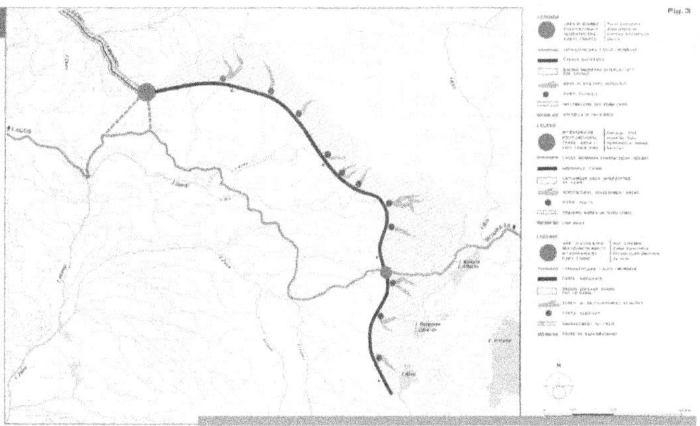

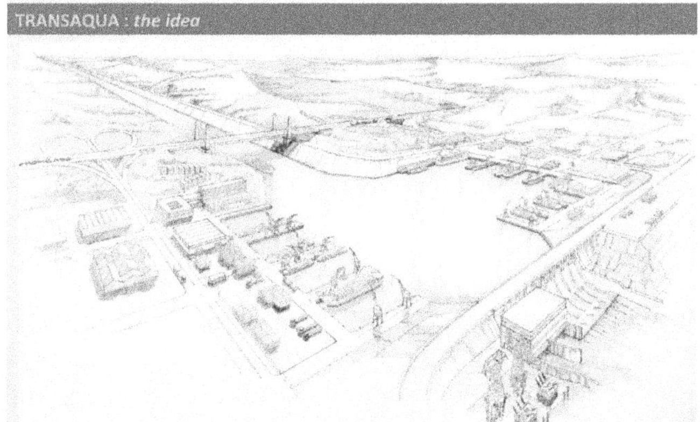

Well, water transfer to drying up endorheic lakes is not merely a "nature conservation measure." Environment and wildlife deserve to be protected—human beings, too. A drying endorheic lake is proof that the water resources in its catchment area are overexploited with respect to incoming run-off. Transfering water from adjacent river basins that have surplus water flowing into the sea, is a way of increasing water availability, especially for agriculture, in the context of the increasing population and declining rainfall, and to restore wildlife.

When water is in short supply in a given place, either you bring it there, or people will migrate elsewhere.

Near Lake Chad, there is an immense, scarcely populated river basin, which discharges into the Atlantic Ocean an average of 40,000 cubic meters/second—the equivalent to 1,250 billion m^3/year. That discharge is 200 times the discharge of the Main River [in Germany], or 14 times that of the Rhine at its mouth. How much of this volume could be possibly and safely di-

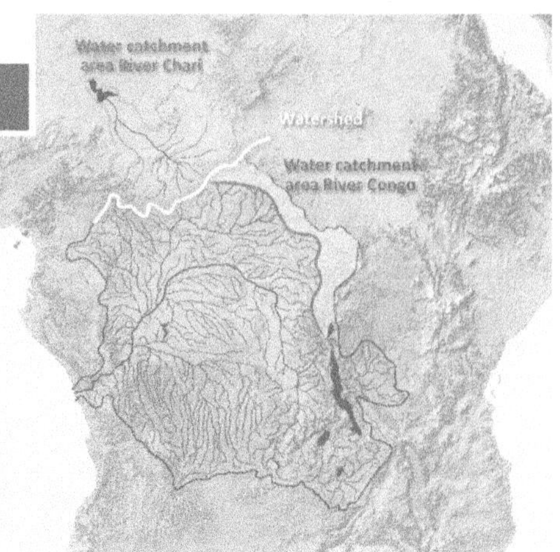

That this less than 8% of the Congo discharge, ensuring thus the restoration of Lake Chad and irrigation of up to 3 million hectares.

In its fall toward Chad, the diverted flow could be used for hydropower production. Along the canal, a road should be built which would become the backbone of inter-African land transport. The hypothesis that the canal could also be suitable for navigation has been made. Those ideas stemming from the early 1920s, have been studied by Bonifica, and are presently being considered by the Lake Chad Basin Commission as a possible project for the future.

The idea of Bonifica is to transfer about 100 million cubic meters of water per year from the Congo River Basin to the Lake Chad and Sahel district. This is the Congo Basin as you can see in red, which is the alignment more or less of the canal. You cross the watershed and you go into the water catchment area of the River Chari.

What is important to note is that the Transaqua formula is not simply to replenish Lake Chad, but to give access to drinking water, revive agricultural activity, irrigation, fish farming, a navigable waterway, trade, transport, regulate flows, produce electric power, river ports, commerce, and road connections—thus creating an economic development system along the Transaqua waterway.

With the regeneration of Lake Chad's natural resources, we can show the shape of the lake in 2087. Characteristic of this project is that navigable infrastructure systems can be realized through modules. We don't need to realize the whole project at the same time, so we start from the part which is most near to the watershed, and the development of the first 500 km of the canal.

The Transaqua water project is a combination of situations. In order to produce hydropower, we will con-

verted into Lake Chad has yet to be studied.

Can we think of a "win-win" project, where all countries involved have their advantages, which is perhaps, one of the basic conditions for developing this project?

Bringing water from the Congo River Basin to the thirsty Chad region and increasing irrigated agriculture, restoring the lake, producing hydropower and improving inter-African transport and commerce, is the vision of this Transaqua Project.

A canal would have to intercept part of the discharge of the right-hand tributaries of the Congo River, and convey them across the watershed between the Congo Basin and the Chari Basin. The diverted flow would reach Lake Chad through one of the Chari tributaries, properly reshaped. A very preliminary estimate gives an amount up to 100 billion m³/year could be diverted.

struct small dams along the tributaries of the river, in order to catch some part of the water for the Transaqua canal. By connecting different lakes with canals, we can realize a waterway which will have a maximum extent of up to 2,400 km, reaching Lake Tanganyika on the east side of Africa.

Road connection: As you can see, the Transaqua corridor intersects the Lagos-Mombasa Road, which is one of the principal roads that was shown by Profes-

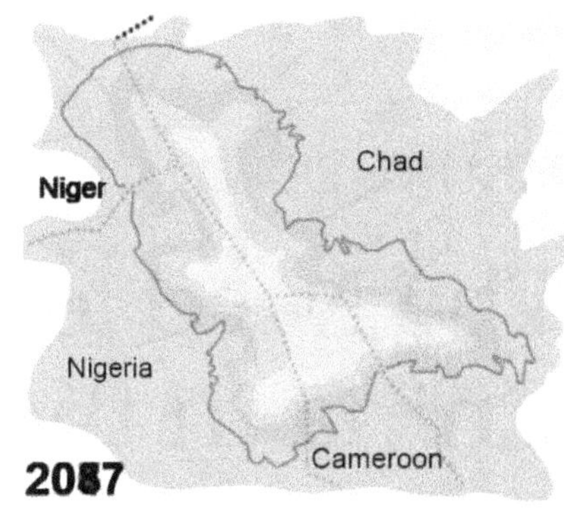

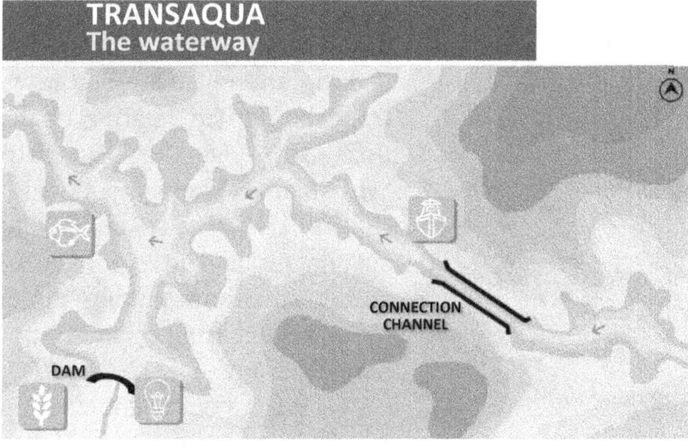

sor Askary in his speech. And as you can see, in the Mombasa-Nairobi link, it is one of the hubs of the One Belt, One Road project.

It is very interesting to think that this Transaqua Project can become one of the projects that can be developed within the One Belt, One Road project.

Some final considerations: Having for years pursued a dream, now is the time to take action. From this point of view, what is interesting and new is the fact that the Chinese have begun to get interested in the project. Last year, a Memorandum of Understanding (MOU) was signed between the Lake Chad Basin Commission, and ChinaPower, which is one of the big infrastructure companies of China. The scope of the MOU was to start the feasibility study of the water transfer project, by trying to construct one of the first elements of the project, which is the CIMA Project. I don't have time now to explain this CIMA project, but it is certainly one of the modules of Transaqua, although it is only part of it, because the CIMA project, developed by the Canadian CIMA company, is a project to pump water from the

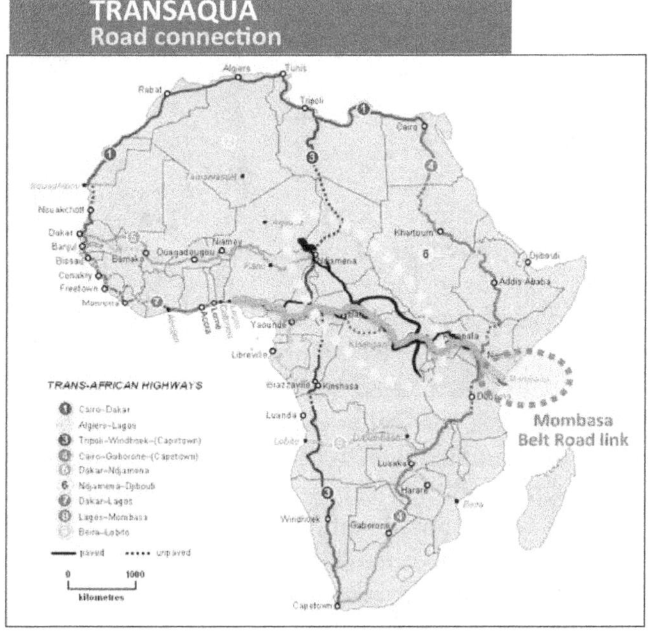

Ubangi River over the watershed into the Chari River, which is a different vision from Transaqua, which is to construct a corridor crossing Africa, and bringing development to all the regions that are crossed by the project.

It is important at this point to show that Bonifica, in the context of the signing of this MOU, decided to go to China and to speak to ChinaPower, in order to offer the collaboration of Europeans, of Italians, to jointly develop the feasibility study. We found a great interest from the Chinese, so we signed an MOU and now we are taking action in order to jointly develop this feasibility project together with the Chinese. This may be the first break in the construction of this important infrastructure in the center of Africa.

Thank you. [applause]

MEHRETEAB MULUGETA

The Need for Europe to Cooperate with China in the Industrialization of Africa

Mr. Mehreteab Mulugeta Haile is Consul General of Ethiopia in Frankfurt. This is an edited transcript of his address to the International Schiller Institute conference on "Fulfilling the Dream of Mankind," Nov. 25-26, 2017, in Bad Soden/Taunus, Germany. Subtitles have been added.

Mrs. Helga Zepp-La-Rouche, President and Founder of the Schiller Institute, distinguished participants, ladies and gentlemen, at the outset, allow me to thank and express my appreciation to the Schiller Institute for organizing conferences that help shed light on current political and economic developments in the world. I feel honored and I am thankful to be invited and to make a speech at this august gathering.

Today, I will talk about Ethiopia's rapid economic development and its involvement in regional cooperation, and contributions made by Europe and China to enhance these developments.

Ethiopia is one of the largest Least Developed Countries (LDCs) in Sub-Saharan Africa, with a population of about 100 million people. After suffering economic stagnation for decades, its economy began to grow in the mid-1990s after a new administration led by the Ethiopian People's Revolutionary Democratic Front (EPRDF) took the helm of government.

For the last 15 years, Ethiopia has become one of the fastest growing economies in the world, with an average Gross Domestic Product (GDP) growth rate of about 11% per annum. To continue with this rapid economic growth, the Ethiopian Government rolled out, in 2010, an ambitious five-year Growth and Transforma-

Mehreteab Mulugeta Haile

tion Plan (GTP) that aims to attain a lower-middle-income status by 2025. Currently the country is implementing the second Growth and Transformation Plan (GTP II), which is built on Sectoral Policies, Strategies & Program and Lessons drawn from the implementation of the first GTP and the post-2015 "sustainable development goals" (SDGs). It has also taken into account global and regional economic situations having direct or indirect bearing on the Ethiopian economy.

GTP II aims, for the coming 8 to 10 years, to continue achieving an annual average real GDP growth rate of 11% within a stable macroeconomic environment, while at the same time pursuing aggressive measures towards rapid industrialization and structural transformation. To this end, concerted and coordinated effort will be made so that equitable economic growth translates into creating job opportunities accompanied by significant poverty reduction. Agriculture will be maintained as a major source of growth, while the development of industries by accelerating industrial development will be supplemented with the promotion of the service sector, so as to enhance growth. To this effect, coordinated and strong forward and backward production linkages will be strengthened. Private sector investment will be promoted through providing the necessary incentives and support, to enhance private sector participation in allowed investment areas.

Expansion of infrastructure development—such as road, railway, dry port, air transport, energy, telecommunications, water, and irrigation schemes—will have special consideration in GTP II.

Xinhua/Michael Tewelde

Construction at the Hawassa Industrial Park built by China Civil Engineering Corporation, Feb. 3, 2016.

Industry and Infrastructure Development

During GTP II, industrial development and structural transformation is expected to bring significant growth of the manufacturing industry, so that it plays the leading role in the overall economic development of the country. Implementation strategies mainly focus on implementation of projects and programs which are geared towards attracting quality investment, enhancing production and productivity, boosting export shares, accelerating technological learning, and strengthening the linkage among industries. To this end, establishing 12 industrial parks and clusters has been undertaken in the country, with 7 million square meters of land made available for investors engaged in manufacturing and related sectors. Four agro-industrial parks will also be established which will be linked with millions of smallholder farmers supplying input. Regional administrative areas, cities and towns will get the necessary support to develop standardized industrial clusters and parks for those investors promoting small to medium-size industries, and hence generate employment opportunities.

Expanding the manufacturing sector will focus on identifying new investment areas such as biotechnology, petrochemicals, electricity and electronics, information and communication technologies (hardware and software production industries).

In the infrastructure sector, the overall strategic direction is to ensure the creation of infrastructure that supports rapid economic growth and structural transformation. This direction will create mass employment opportunities, an institution having strong implementa-

tion capacity, ensure public participation and benefit, construct decentralized infrastructure development systems, solve financial constraints, ensure fairness and profitability, and ensure integrated planning and administration of infrastructure development.

Within infrastructure overall, rural roads are given high focus—to help reduce poverty by facilitating easy access of agricultural products, at low transportation cost, to the market, improving access to basic socioeconomic services, and strengthening rural-urban linkages.

Thus, the major strategic directions of the road development sector during GTP II will be ensuring the existence and sustainability of road infrastructure network with quality and safety, as well as to improve the provision of road infrastructure, by expanding the road network both in terms of quantity and quality, to sustain and ensure current and future economic growth.

The other area that has been given major emphasis is the energy sector. The main objective of the sector during GTP II is increasing national energy generation, transmission, and distribution capacity to fully satisfy domestic energy demand with production surplus ready for the export market. Implementation strategies are set, to increase electric power generating capacity through initiatives in hydro power, wind power, geothermal power, and solar power.

The other major project in the area of infrastructure building is railway development. The major strategic direction of railways infrastructure development during GTP II is to continue the network expansion started under GTP I, build capacity by establishing a modern railway industry academy, and make it operational; develop various railway industry standards; ensure that railway transport services are in accordance with standards, and conduct problem solving research on railway infrastructure building, operations, and service provision.

The objectives of the construction industry during the GTP II period are to build the capacity of the industry in a sustainable way, ensure the efficiency and effectiveness of construction procurement and contract management, develop internationally competent contractors and design & construction consultants, and improve the availability of construction raw materials and machinery for those engaged in construction and housing development programs.

Regional and International Development

We in Ethiopia believe that economic development in a secluded situation cannot be sustainable and attainable. To this end, Ethiopia, through the Intergovernmental Authority for Development (IGAD), is increasingly collaborating with its neighbors—notably Kenya, Sudan, Djibouti, Sudan, and South Sudan—in the areas of trade, tourism, industry, infrastructure development, and energy, among others. The Ethiopian private sector is increasingly encouraged to invest in those countries and all these countries are thus enhancing their economic cooperation. We in Ethiopia are striving to bring regional economic integration to create a larger regional market for trade and investment and make use of the advantages of efficiency, productivity gains, and competitiveness. In recent years the Ethiopian government has taken steps to enhance non-trade aspects of economic cooperation, which could strengthen economic ties among the countries in the region.

Xinhua/Sun Ruibo
A new train at a railway station in Addis Abeba, Ethiopia, Oct. 1, 2016.

Xinhua
Chinese locomotive driver Liu Ji (R) trains his Ethiopian counterparts at a railway station in suburban Addis Ababa, Ethiopia, Oct 1, 2016.

IGAD's focus on regional economic cooperation and integration is to create an open, unified, regional economic space for the business community—a single market open to competitive entry and well integrated into the continental and global economies. This focus requires both regional infrastructure as well as the gradual harmonization of policies for the removal of barriers to inter-state communications.

The European Union and other development partners are actively supporting and participating in economic development activities in Ethiopia. Through its development cooperation, the EU stands by Ethiopia in addressing its key challenges, such as food insecurity, rapidly growing population, environmental pressures exacerbated by climate change, low industrial output, and a range of governance issues. In recent years, the EU+ group disbursed annually around 1 billion euros in official development assistance (ODA), equivalent to roughly a quarter of the total external aid to Ethiopia, and it may reach up to 10% of the country's annual federal budget in certain years. In this context, joint programming is not only about aid effectiveness, but most importantly, has a strong political dimension and is one of the instruments in support of the implementation of the wider EU-Ethiopia strategic engagement. The European Union supports the efforts of Ethiopia to eradicate poverty, and to foster inclusive and sustainable economic, social, and environmental development while promoting human rights, democracy, and other elements of good governance.

For the last three years, much focus has been given to the issue of migration and its management by European countries. Ethiopia is a key partner in the stability and management of migratory flows in the region, due to its role in hosting large numbers of refugees from neighboring countries, its proactive policy of fighting traffickers and smugglers, and the interest of Ethiopians in migrating to neighboring countries and regions in search of work. Ethiopia is one of the five priority countries identified in the Communication on Establishing a

New Partnership Framework with Third Countries under the European Agenda on Migration. Through the EU Trust Fund for Africa, EU actions address the root causes of irregular migration in the most migrant-prone regions of the country, promoting economic and employment opportunities, particularly for vulnerable people, through vocational training, access to micro-finance, or by creating industrial parks. Actions also aim to strengthen resilience and combat the drivers of instability, to improve long-term development and protection needs of refugees and their host communities, and to better manage migration at regional level.

When we look at the role Germany is playing in the relationship of African countries with EU countries, in general, and Ethiopia in particular, we find that Germany has made cooperation with Africa a core element of its G-20 Presidency. The German government advocates for a G-20 Africa Partnership and has put in place the G-20 Compact with Africa, which aims to promote private investment, sustainable infrastructure, and job creation in African countries. Germany's Minister of Finance describes the Compact with Africa as a "long-term, demand-driven process" in which "African countries will determine what they want to do to improve conditions for private investment, with whom they want to cooperate, and in what form."

China and Africa

Last year, during its G-20 Presidency, China made Africa a prominent part of the G-20 agenda, with an unprecedented number of African leaders participating in the G-20 Summit in Hangzhou and with commitments to support industrialization and the proliferation of renewable energy in African countries.

According to data from China's Ministry of Commerce (MOFCOM), the stock of Chinese direct investment in Africa was $32 billion at the end of 2014. Of course, direct investment is not the only form of foreign financing. The Export-Import Bank of China and China Development Bank have made large loans in Africa, mostly to fund infrastructure projects. In recent years, China has provided about one-sixth of the external infrastructure financing for Africa. In short, Chinese financing is substantial enough to contribute meaning-

Xinhua/Sun Ruibo

People in line for newly opened passenger rail station in Addis Abeba, Ethiopia, Sept. 20, 2015.

fully to African investment and growth. However, the notion that China has provided an overwhelming amount of finance and is buying up the whole continent is inaccurate.

If we take my country, Ethiopia, as an example of Chinese cooperation and involvement in Africa, we find that what has been said above is false. According to the Ethiopian Investment Commission, Chinese companies, with close to 379 projects that were either operational or under implementation in the 2012-2017 period, are on top of Ethiopia's investment landscape, both in number and financial capital. Among these companies, 279 were operational with projects that are worth over 13.16 billion Ethiopian birr (over 572 million U.S. dollars) during the reported period, while the remaining 100 are under implementation.

In terms of employment creation, Chinese companies have created more than 28,300 jobs in various sectors in Ethiopia during the reported period, of which over 19,000 were created in Ethiopia's manufacturing, as it is the leading sector in attracting companies from China. China brings not only investment, knowhow, and transfer of technology, but also skills and entrepreneurship.

At this point, I would like to mention the initiative taken by His Excellency President Xi Jinping in 2013, the "One Belt, One Road" (OBOR) Initiative. This is President Xi's "project of the century." It is based on the legendary Silk Road, which connected Europe and China for one and a half millennia. The aim of China's OBOR project is to open up and expand old Silk Road trade routes through Central Asia and on to Europe, as well as Southeast Asian maritime links through the Strait of Malacca and around India to the Middle East. Xi's ambitious goals do sound inspiring indeed: "We should build the Belt and Road into a road of peace … of prosperity … of opening up … of innovation … connecting civilizations," he said. The total trade between China and other Belt and Road countries has exceeded $3 trillion. China's investment has surpassed $50 billion. Chinese companies have created almost 200,000 jobs and over $1 billion of tax revenue. China is generating mutual benefits by creating jobs and supporting the domestic economy of those countries in which it is investing.

The Jamestown Foundation's *China Brief* stated this month (paraphrase):

> OBOR will bring a greater effect on local and regional integration along the way, especially for Ethiopia and other countries in the region. The Maritime Silk Road will have a significant impact both because of economic integration on a local level, and by forging connections between East Africa and neighboring regions. It also connects regional centers to each other. OBOR could partly ease a problem that has bedevilled African development since the end of the colonial era. It also has the potential to facilitate trade and shared manufacturing between different East African economies. In this sense, the OBOR initiative has the potential to achieve a certain amount of regional integration—a long-held ideal of African development. OBOR presents an intriguing perspective on the sometimes highly unequal nature of south-south cooperation, and raises questions about the nature of African agency in the 21st Century.

German-Chinese-African Development

It is estimated that Africa needs to create about 20 million jobs per year to employ its expanding workforce. Africa's demographics present both an opportunity and a challenge to the rest of the world. It is unrealistic to expect Europe or China to tackle the problems of African countries alone and bring a change overnight. Nor would it be reasonable to expect large volumes of Chinese or European manufacturing to move to the continent in the near future. Therefore, it is useful to have a long-term vision of economic relationship that very much centers on the utilization of natural resources of Africa and the shift over time to a greater focus on human resources development by creating jobs. To this end, trilateral cooperation would provide an ideal opportunity for Germany and China, as the current and previous G-20 Presidencies, to jointly demonstrate their commitments under the G-20 to increase support for African countries. This form of cooperation complements and brings together the traditional North-South and South-South cooperation models. In line with the Compact with Africa, such cooperation needs to be guided by the African Union's Agenda 2063 and African countries' national development plans in order to be successful.

The launch of the Sino-German Center for Sustainable Development in Beijing in May is a promising step in this direction, as the center plans to support sustainable infrastructure development in African countries. This can, indeed, be an area in which African countries can benefit from joint cooperation between Germany and China. China has a comparative advantage in the provision of cost-effective infrastructure development, while the sustainability of such projects can be ensured by making use of Germany's expertise in project management, social and environmental impact assessments, and quality assurance.

Germany and China should also foster trilateral cooperation with African countries on industrialization and renewable energy. The joint establishment of special economic zones (SEZs) in African countries would be a good starting point. SEZs were a key component of China's economic development and are also starting to play an important role for industrialization in African countries such as Ethiopia. A trilateral SEZ project should utilize China's profound experience in financing, developing, and managing SEZs, while Germany would contribute its expertise in preparing and delivering tailored technical vocational education and training programs for different sectors. Germany's understanding of social and environmental standards and its international marketing insights would also help ensure that SEZs are attractive for investors and suitable for global supply chains.

There is also a huge potential for effective trilateral cooperation between Germany, China, and African countries on the proliferation of renewable energy in Africa. The African Union's recently launched Africa Renewable Energy Initiative (AREI) provides a possible entry point, as both China and Germany have individually pledged their support for the initiative. Both countries are global leaders in renewable energy policy and technology, and have considerable experience working with African countries bilaterally in these areas. A trilateral project should focus on a so far overlooked, but crucial component in the establishment of the Africa Renewable Energy Institute, namely, to serve as the initiative's backbone for research and training. Germany and China could build on the experiences from the establishment and operation of similar institutes in China, such as the China-EU Institute for Clean and Renewable Energy, and engage these institutes and their networks to build new partnerships. Thank you.

MONI ABDULLAH

Egypt's 2030 Mega Projects: Investment Opportunities for Intermodal and Multimodal Connectivity

This is an edited transcript of a presentation by Mrs. Moni Abdullah to the Nov. 25-26 Schiller Institute Conference. She is the Executive Manager of Pyramids International, Cairo, Egypt.

HUSSEIN ASKARY: Our next speaker is from Egypt, too: Mrs. Moni Abdullah. She is the General Manager of Pyramids International, which is specialized in arranging international conferences, fairs. But she is passionately advocating the One Belt, One Road, and also Egypt's development programs.

Moni Abdullah

ness to cooperate with the New Silk Road Project, for sharing the same courageous spirit of the Egyptians that human reason will be able to find the higher level where problems can be solved, and defending the rights of humanity to progress economically, morally, and intellectually, by development and connectivity.

My children are actually Swiss and I live in Geneva and in Egypt. I would like very much to see connectivity through Egypt to all of Africa, and possibly for the three continents to connect Europe, Africa, and Asia.

MRS. MONI ABDULLAH: Good afternoon. Ladies and Gentlemen, Distinguished Guests, Dear Friends:

My name is Moni Abdullah. I am the general manager of Pyramids International group, which is a private sector company. First I would like to express my gratitude and appreciation to be invited as a speaker today at such an important event. I would further extend my gratitude to the Schiller Institute, and Mrs. Helga Zepp-LaRouche in particular, for taking an interest in our company and in Egypt, and in an initiative and willing-

Our company is an events organizer. We organize conferences and exhibitions worldwide. We are an ISO-certified company and accredited with UFI, the global association of the exhibition industry.

Pyramids International group was established in 1993 and specializes in organizing, planning, and holding all kinds of large-scale international activities, such as conference, exhibitions, and trade shows. We work with different sectors, and organize around 115 events worldwide, basically in oil and gas, energy, and renewable energy, transportation, maritime and ports, ship-

President El-Sisi addressing the Suez Canal Global conference on Feb. 24, 2016.

This is the Suez Canal parallel dredging waterway canal. It's a megaproject that was concluded in one year, to increase the depth of the canal and to have a double, parallel waterway. It reduces the time of transport, for example, from Asia to Europe, and it reduces the cost as well. It can now accommodate the biggest vessels, thanks to its greater depth. These are some photos of the different container ships. That is the Suez Canal Economic Zone, or corridor.

The conference we organized, was to market the megaprojects in Egypt, for international investors who would like to engage in the megaprojects taking place. The megaprojects taking place are in different sectors, and as Mr. Hussein kindly mentioned, Egypt wants to leap to develop, we don't want to crawl; so in parallel, there are megaprojects in transport, in industry, in agriculture and so on.

The Suez Canal Global Conference was followed by a Suez Canal tour, where the attendees could come and engage in debates, discussing the maritime field, and ping, and logistics, fashion, leather, furniture, health, real estate, general trade shows, auto shows, building and construction, household, food, machinery, and more.

In the continuous development of its business the company has established wide cooperation and interactive relations with the related governmental departments, trade associations, nongovernmental organizations, and scientific research institutes.

As a diversified service company, it also offers media services, digital information consulting services, research capacity and marketing solutions. Hence, our database marketing capacity and business connections help our worldwide international customers do business and to succeed in reaching new markets.

We organized the First Suez Canal Global Conference, last February, under the patronage of His Excellency President Abdel Fattah el-Sisi, the Egyptian President. Here are some photos of the exhibition and the conference at the same time.

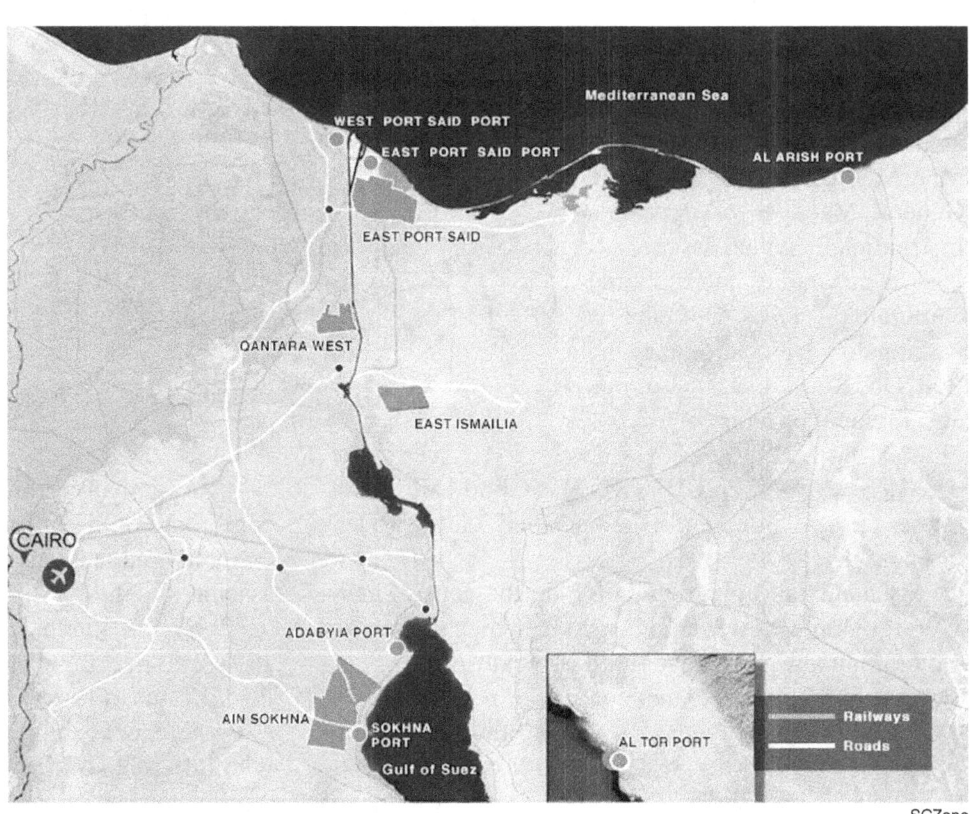

Suez Canal Economic Zone overview.

then go on a tour of the Suez Canal to see it in reality.

The function of our conferences was to foster discussions of a variety of issues affecting the Suez Canal and its development, clarify the opportunities for investment, the role of the megaprojects, and how it will serve to boost the traffic handled by the canal. The Conference aimed to help develop a Suez Canal Zone area, transforming it into a world-class global logistic hub and industrial processing center to serve the global market.

cc/Hajotthu

Enrance to the Suez Canal at Port Said.

The importance and invention of the Suez Canal: The Suez Canal is considered to be shortest link between east and west, compared with the Cape of Good Hope. Due to its unique geographic locale, it's an important international navigational canal, linking the Mediterranean Sea at Port Said and the Red Sea at Suez.

The distinctive location of the Suez Canal makes it of special significance to the world and to Egypt as well. This importance is augmented with the evolution of maritime transport and world trade. Maritime transport is the cheapest means of transport. More than 80% of the world trade volume via waterways, seaborne. The canal route achieves savings in distance between the ports north and south of the canal, and that is converted into other savings for the shipping industries. These savings are reflected in saving time and saving money. Fuel consumption and operations costs are markedly reduced for vessels that transit the Suez Canal. It's the longest canal in the world without locks, having a high level of safety and security measures, compared to other, alternative routes. Transit navigation there goes on day and night.

The Suez Canal, as I mentioned, accommodates the biggest shipping fleets now. Creating a new canal parallel to the existing one, has maximized benefits from the present canal, and its bypass, doubling the longest possible parts of the waterway, facilitates traffic in the two directions, and minimizing the waiting time for transiting ships. This certainly reduces the time needed for the trip from one end of the canal to the other, and increase the numerical capacity of the waterway, In anticipation of the expected growth in world trade.

The project goes hand in hand with the Suez Canal area development project. The two projects will add to the importance of the Suez Canal and will make it the route of choice for shipowners the world over, putting any alternative routes out of competition—hopefully. The Suez Canal Area Development Project is now a preferential market, because of the bilateral and multilateral agreements that Egypt benefits from, with Africa, with the Middle East, with Europe, and with the U.S.A., through the case agreements, for example; and then extending the operation of this law to the Suez Canal region is an important step towards transforming the Suez Canal to a global trade hub and world trade gateway.

The New Silk Road is an enormous Chinese project, which has gone global. It is composed of land routes, known as the Silk Road Economic Belt, and sea routes known as the 21st-Century Maritime Silk Road, and both pass, actually, through the Suez Canal. It goes to Nairobi, Kenya and then afterwards to the Suez Canal. Together they make up the One Belt, One Road, creating a link among the three continents.

Egypt has taken steps forwards towards the New Silk Road global vision: The New Silk Road will boost trade, productivity, investment, and cultural exchange, of course.

The 21st-Century Maritime Silk Road crosses the Indian Ocean, and then it goes through the Suez Canal. The Suez Canal Corridor Area Project is a megaproject in Egypt that has been launched by President Abdel Fattah el-Sisi. The project's aim is to increase the role of the Suez Canal region in international trading, and to develop the three canal cities located around it. The project involves building a new city, Ismailia, and fish farms, industrial zones, technology valleys, seven new tunnels—many, many, many megaprojects that Dr. Saad Elgioshy, former Egyptian transport minister mentioned before.

Building on that, the project will transform the canal cities into important trading centers globally. The purpose of this project is to make the region a global industrial center and a logistics services and maritime transport hub, making the Suez Canal a world trade gateway between east and west.

A number of key priorities are identified, including the Port Said port, which aims to develop all of the ports, logistics services, maritime activities and an industrial cluster on the eastern side of the canal. In addition, there are port expansion projects— expansion of Port Said West Port, Ras Sadr Port, and many other ports.

And then there's Ismailia Technology Valley, establishing high-tech projects in the fields of electronics, communications, IT, biotechnology, medical components, and pharma-technology.

And then northwest of the Gulf of Suez, the project comprises a large industrial zone in close proximity to Ras Sadr Port covering 200 km, including industrial parks and many previously mentioned megaprojects.

Investment opportunities. And this is why I'm here: Egypt is has many opportunities for investment in different ways, with the government, or with the private sector. As previously mentioned by former Egyptian Minister Dr. Saad, Egypt is offering for the first time opportunities for development and investment in the long-term plan, to transform Egypt 2013 to a leading country in the region, a major global trading hub, and place it as a landmark on the global investment map as one of the most promising and attractive countries for investment in logistics and transport sectors. Many of its future multi-billion-dollar national projects rank it third in the Middle East and Africa region, in terms of the volume of investment availability. Egypt will also take offers for global and domestic investment in existing and prospective projects starting soon in various sectors within the medium-term plan until 2020, with investment exceeding 300 billion Egyptian pounds.

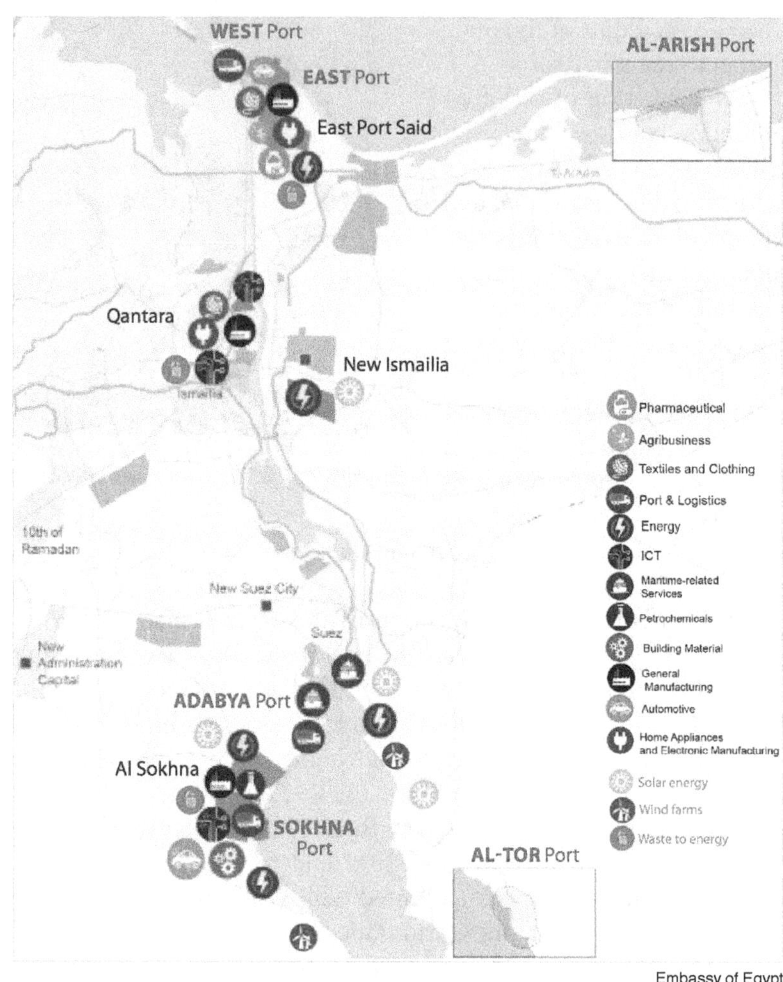

Embassy of Egypt

The Suez Canal Economic Zone.

One of the most important topics of the conference was to discuss the investment opportunities in the New Silk Road, to enable Egypt to link between the continents of Asia, Europe, and Africa, to create new opportunities for countries with development wishes. Egypt has taken steps forward towards a global vision and has already signed contracts with the Chinese government for cooperation on Egyptian railway projects, because the New Silk Road promotes trade, productivity, investment, and cultural exchange.

TEDA, which is the Chinese-Suez Economic and Trade Cooperation Zone based in the Suez Canal Economic Zone, is a fine example of how the Chinese are engaged in Egypt, and is actually considered to be one of the best overseas economic and trade cooperation zones of China. It has established a good overseas development platform for Chinese enterprises, going global with the aim of creating an international capacity cooperation model of how the overseas economic and trade cooperation zones can be "win-win" situations.

Any manufacturer based in the Suez Canal Economic Zone has so many facilities and incentives to benefit from. For example now, Egypt is making many reforms, such as the new investment law, with "one-stop shop"—better licensing procedures, faster, you don't have to go through government bureaucracy any more to get licensing. Also there is the floatation of the Egyptian currency, so now there's no black market—there's one currency rate. There are bilateral agreements and the multilateral agreements, as I mentioned before, and many industrial areas and free zones available.

There's a lot of legislative reform and social reform going on as well in Egypt.

Now, I would like to talk about our upcoming events in the transport sector: for whoever is interested in participating and learning more about the megaprojects that are taking place there, and how Egypt is trying to connect the three continents.

We are having one on April 16-17: It's called the 2030 Megaprojects and it's about means of transport in Egypt.

In tandem with the conference, there will be two exhibitions: Pharos, the International Exhibition of Maritime Transport Logistics and Shipping; and the Middle East and Africa Rail Show, the International Exhibition for Railway Systems Underground Metro and Mass Transportation. The conference and two exhibitions are being organized by our company. The conference with its two international exhibitions will be a very important event for investors, developers, professionals, and stakeholders as the Egyptian Ministry of Transport will present, for the first time, a comprehensive vision of its entire plan for megaprojects in inter-modal and multi-modal transportation connecting Egypt locally and internationally, based on Egypt's strategic location, linking Africa, Europe, and Asia, and the Middle East, of course, all in accordance with the strategy of sustainable development, the vision Egypt 2030.

The conference will be a global gathering for international experts from the east and west, with the support of many international organizations, associations, financial authorities, and government entities around the world.

Xinhua/Ju Peng

President Xi Jinping (right) meets President Abdel-Fattah El-Sisi at the Dialogue of Emerging Markets and Developing countries on Sept. 5, 2017, in China.

Egypt now is trying to develop its rail system, as we said. Years of underdevelopment, and now, all of a sudden, there is a boost in all of the transport sectors. We're trying to have an efficient railway system that connects Egypt internally, supported by good, proper service for truck fleets, and increasing river transport services, and development in all of the ports and the logistics centers. So Egypt will have a complete, new network, which is safe, reduces cost, and is efficient. That will enable Egypt to be able to connect internationally. Egypt-based manufacturers in the new industrial areas can actually reduce the cost of transfer and the time of products to the three different continents.

Egypt is trying to brand itself and position itself to be a world trade hub. The objective of Pharos is to emphasize the role of the private sector and investment in maritime transport and logistics, multimodal transport and logistics centers in the Arab region in Africa, and the role of dryland and river ports and logistics centers in supporting and developing the economy, elaborating the role and use of information technology, and infrastructure in the maritime transport sector, and intensifying the role of green ports and its impact on the environment.

Following Pharos, we will have the Middle East and Africa Exhibition for Infrastructure, underground roads, bridges, transportation. And in cooperation with the Schiller Institute, we will have the EWTH, Egypt World Trade Hub East and West Connectivity conference, proposed for July. That conference will focus on Egypt being a good and desirable place for world trade connectivity, and not only between East and West, but also between the northern and southern regions of Africa.

Egypt World Trade Hub is connecting east and west is proposed to take place in July. It will discuss development investment opportunities in Egypt's infrastructure, railways, roads, underground bridges, tunnels in land transport, ports, logistics centers, maritime and shipping services, all transforming Egypt into a major world-class trade hub, and placing it on the map of one of the top potential investment countries in the logistics and transport sectors. Due to its strategic location, Egypt aims to connect the Middle East and Africa, Europe, and Asia, to become a prominent leader in the new era. The conference will discuss the Marshall Plan of intermodal and multimodal connectivity of Egypt to the three continents.

The Egypt World Trade Hub Conference will discuss ways of connecting and increasing global trade, examining latest trends in global trade with an outlook on alternative routes, and discussing the importance of Egypt's strategic location that connects the three continents. Panel discussions will cover Egypt's local and foreign investment opportunities in Egyptian industrial areas, free trade zones, and all of the Egyptian transport sectors that are witnessing major expansion and development, creating a wider vista of commerce for Africa, Europe, and Asia.

Inviting investors and developers to relocate to Egypt to benefit from the many incentives and facilities, Egypt is now offering and benefitting from the reduction in cargo transport costs and transfer time, by the parallel way dredging megaproject of the Suez Canal. Egypt is pursuing existing means that encourage export to east and west, and the whole region, acting as a great big hub for logistics and world trade.

China and Egypt agreed to cooperate on the New Silk Road and signed a five-year agreement to that end, calling for redoubled efforts to develop the China-Egypt Suez Economic and Trade Cooperation Zone. Egypt has taken steps toward a global vision, and has already signed agreements and contracts with the Chinese government. [applause]

For more details, there are brochures at the table in the back of the conference hall and outside at the registration area for the 2030 Megaprojects and for the Egypt World Trade Hub conference.

Thank you very much.

July 7, 1999

Prometheus and Europe

by Lyndon H. LaRouche, Jr.

The U.S.A. will not be capable of choosing those decisions on which its survival now depends, unless there is, now, a rapidly renewed influence of Classical thinking. This renewal must occur within a citizenry which had become, predominately, disastrously illiterate, and often wildly irrational, even relative to the standards of twenty-five years ago. The strategic purpose of the present, like related earlier reports, is to prompt those who are able, to educate broader circles among their fellow-citizens. Their task, like that of *EIR*, is to communicate ideas which must become influential, if this nation is to outlive the presently accelerating global crisis.

Effecting such a result, within the relatively short time now available, will not seem an impossible chore to those who are encouraged, as I am, by study of similar efforts in the Americas, and elsewhere, during certain critical earlier periods of, in particular, U.S. and European history.

The required method, is the same method used successfully during the middle to late Eighteenth Century, by our Benjamin Franklin, and by Lessing and Moses Mendelssohn in Europe, and by the Fifteenth Century Renaissance, earlier. The method is based on provoking not only prominent, but also so-called ordinary people, into facing those facts which force them to overcome the ignorance which has been recently, habitually embedded in them. The ignorance which must be overcome, is typified by present-day, widely and strongly held, but destructive popular prejudices. The proven method, from those cited and other notable cases of cultural renaissances from past history, is the method which *EIR* is applying to this work today.

The policy is, to educate a small minority of the citizens, who will, in turn, educate others, who will, in turn, educate still more. We should recognize, from comparable, successful experiences of the past, that those who participate in learning to teach others, in this chain-letter sort of organizing process, will be, together with their children, among the leading citizens of our republic during the years to come. That happy outcome assumes, of course, that our republic survives the presently ongoing succession of crises, that during the months preceding the next U.S. general election.

The principal obstacle preventing such happy results earlier during recent times, has been that such a proposed, rapid success, in bringing up the level of the morality and intellect of an entire people, occurs only as the poet Percy Shelley described this process, in his celebrated *In Defence of Poetry*. In ordinary times, such an uplifting of the intellectual and moral level of even a small portion of the population, often appears to be a thankless, if necessary, tiresome drudgery, an effort enjoyed only by a few stubbornly exceptional thinkers and their pupils. Only under special conditions of profound crisis among nations, as now, do the preconditions exist, for a sudden upsurge of the general power of people *for receiving and imparting, profound and impassioned conceptions, respecting man and nature.*[1]

At present, the world as a whole is gripped by one of history's greatest instances of the kind of period of

---

1. "A Defence of Poetry," ***Shelley's Poetry and Prose: Authoritative Text, Criticism*** (New York: W.W. Norton and Co., 1977). Shelley himself emphasized that John Keats was the greater master as a poet; but it was Shelley who helped us better to understand the genius expressed by Keats.

rising crisis to which Shelley referred. During recent months, especially since the past Winter's mad effort to carry out a political lynching of President Clinton, and since the associated succession of financial crisis and war which followed the Washington G-7 meeting of last October, the political and economic situation now deteriorates at an accelerating rate. As a result of this turn, there has been a perceptible, now accelerating quickening of the minds, spreading among more strata of the population. More and more of an increasingly fearful population smells the approaching death of the existing economic order. It smells that odor of doom emanating, world-wide, from the proverbial "old regimes." In past history, this kind of window of opportunity now opening up, has been small. In such brief intervals as this one, we must then soon seize that opportunity, or lose it forever.

Any alert, reasonably well-informed observer, can see such a crisis, erupting, as if seismically, around the world today. If, and only if, that relatively brief opportunity is seized appropriately, and quickly enough, our nation can, and will land safely on the safer, far side of the presently rising storm. Otherwise, past comparable periods of history should have forewarned you, that without using that approach, of which this present report is an integral part, this nation will not survive during your children's lifetimes.

If you had any doubt that our nation has been sinking into a quicksand of functional illiteracy, ask: What percentile of the pupils in local schools are being turned into virtual zombies, even killers, by programs of stuffing the pupils with the disassociative, mind-deadening drugs, such as Ritalin, Prozac, and dexedrine, and so-called "information," instead of knowledge? What does that tell you about the kind of education being delivered to those victims, those pupils, by our schools, and by the Internet?

Ask, then: Is the content of mass media output much better, or, perhaps, even worse, than that destruction of our young, presently ongoing within our schools? Compare today's schoolroom and popular readings with those of twenty-five and fifty years ago. Compare the most popular and other racks of bookstores today, with the offerings of twenty-five and fifty years ago. This nation has adopted many enemies, either real, or merely imagined; the most deadly among the real enemies, is the present "New Age's" spread of illiteracy, and of moral and intellectual numbness, within both the leading ranks of politics and business life, and all ages of the population in general.

How Citizens Fool Themselves

In proceeding as I do now, I forewarn you once more, not to allow yourself to be so microscopically small-minded, as to make the commonplace mistake of recent, increasingly illiterate decades in our nation's life. Do not fool yourself into thinking that the topic presented here is relatively unimportant to the practical side of life in your local community today.

Perhaps some readers will be tempted to think, mistakenly, that I am referring to some "secret doctrine" known only to puppet-masters who control politics on stage from behind the curtain. Those readers should free themselves from such, or similar illusions.

Real politics operates on three levels.

On the lower level of thinking, even that practiced at what most people would consider the levels of high office, ordinary politics operates on the basis of certain relatively superficial, axiomatic presumptions. People, at this lower level, cling to assumptions which operate inside their minds, pretty much as do the definitions, axioms, and postulates of a traditional classroom Euclidean geometry. Most politics—cheap political tricks, for example—functions on the basis of exploiting most people's customary blind faith in those assumptions.

Suddenly, when a crisis like that now erupting world-wide, begins to reshape events, those axiomatic assumptions break down. This is true even for many people in relatively high positions of politics and finance, as today. They are suddenly perplexed by a rapidly changing world. Those changes are being controlled according to new rules they do not understand.

That is what more and more plain citizens, and leading business and political leaders, are discovering now. This will become worse, that rapidly, during the coming weeks and months.

In such times, a new kind of political leadership must emerge. It must replace the style of leadership which was generally accepted, during a period of decades, or even longer, until now. Those who will be effective political and business leaders, under those conditions, will operate on one, or both of two levels of new thinking about policy-making.

On the first of these higher levels, the second level, the new assortment drawn from a retooled combination of both former and new leaders, will simply learn the appropriate new rules, to replace those failed definitions, axioms, and postulates which had seemed to be effective in earlier times.

However, the most effective leaders, will be those who look at this business of political axioms from a still higher, third level. That third level, is represented by those who have come to understand the way in which successive changes in ruling political axioms come about. These are the kinds of thinkers from which the world, in any time, obtains its greatest poets and scientists, and also the best qualified political leaders. This third level represents the quality of leadership which is indispensable for a time of great crises.

It is those other citizens, and their current political leaders, who resist understanding what I have just said in these immediately preceding paragraphs, who will fail us during the presently onrushing world crisis. Like hysterical passengers clinging desperately to what they thought they knew—their failed axioms, their sinking *Titanic*—their leadership, if we permitted it to do so, would take us all down—with the sinking ship.

So, it was, when Abraham Lincoln warned you, that most of our citizens are—as still today—fooled most of the time. He referred to the blind side of those who are so often fooled, because, to speak plainly, they wished to be fooled. Thus, often, in times of crisis, they wish to cling to their blind faith in beliefs which will fail them, even destroy them—as in the case of people occupied in the folly of "financial derivatives" trading today.

The "blind side" of the typical American (among other people), lies in his, or her indifference to subject-matters with which "I don't wish to be bothered." Nothing has caused greater suffering to ninety percent of the people of the U.S.A.—the underdogs—during the past thirty-odd years, than their own desire to limit their at-tention to so-called "practical questions," or, so-called "bread and better" issues of daily life. Usually, it is what they do not wish to see, which hurts them most. Faced with actually important matters, the typical American says, "Please, let's change the subject!"

Thus, disaster creeps up upon them, step by step, always catching them by surprise. That is how they were caught by surprise, by economic disaster which hit the financial markets in October 1987, in October 1997, in October 1998, the Brazil crisis of February 1999, each of which I had forecast beforehand, and also the most recent bail-out crisis of June 1999. In each and all of these cases, the crisis had crept up, year by year, during the past thirty-odd years, to become the situation of ninety percent of the U.S. population today. Now, the "big one" is coming soon, and most people will have said, "No, it won't happen; they [the so-called authorities] would never let it happen!"

Usually, the "blind side" which makes today's all-too-typical U.S. citizen fair prey for fresh disasters, lies within the domain of his customary cynicism, his so-called "popular"—or, *populist*—disdain for principles of science and Classical art. So, we must now do away with populism, and its cult of "libertarianism," and go on to real politics.

In the following pages, I call your attention to one of the most important topics in all political science, the way in which political axioms are radically changed under conditions of severe political and social crisis. See why one of the most powerful political leaders the U.S. has had, operating during a period of the greatest crisis our republic has known up to now, President Abraham Lincoln, taught his Cabinet political lessons of master-politics, passages from the tragedies of William Shakespeare.

Lincoln's celebrated late-night lectures to his war-time Cabinet, on Shakespeare, are not an exception to the kind of practice to be found among the greatest political leaders, in all parts of the world. All of the most successful doctrines of military science, are also derived, and used to be taught, from the standpoint of the Classics, reaching back to ancient Greece. All of the greatest military leaders gained much of their competence in being educated, as masters of real politics, in that way. Much of the knowledge we have about really serious politics, we have from the greatest art inherited from what are sometimes seemingly remote depths of earlier history.

The ancient myth of Prometheus, our subject here,

"President Lincoln's celebrated late-night lectures to his war-time Cabinet, on Shakespeare," writes LaRouche, "are not an exception to the kind of practice to be found among the greatest political leaders, in all parts of the world."

contains one of the most fundamental, and important of those Classical lessons in grand political—and military—strategy.

1. What Art Must Teach Politics

Turn now, once again, to real politics: the nature of man. This time, I present that subject from an indispensable standpoint, the method of Classical artistic principle as such.

As I have stated the reason for this in a recent report: Personalized accounts of experience, on the subject of the elementary form of cognitive relations among groups of individual persons, provide the only mental images by means of which the discovery of validatable, universal artistic, or scientific principles, can be competently reported and argued.[2] Any different sort of discussion of such matters, is merely rhetoric. The difference between the cases of artistic and scientific

principles, is that, whereas the subject of universal physical principles pertains to man's masterful comprehension of the material universe, the subject of universal principles of Classical art, is the individual's explicitly cognitive, rather than sensory, relationship to the sovereign individual cognitive processes of other minds. The clinical evidence of Classical tragedy illustrates this point.[3]

Classical forms of art put human individuals on its stage, and force the meaning of the interrelations so displayed there, to be made visible within the audience's powers of cognitive insight. In this way, Classical art, such as tragedy, impels the individual members of the audience, to experience a prescience of the pairwise cognitive interactions of the deepest interior of those minds presented on stage.[4]

Successful such artistic compositions, force the mind in the audience, to look beyond the diversions of sense-certainty. They shift the audience's focus, to insight into the seemingly spiritual, shaping, orbital force exerted over the drama's battlefields. They show, thus, how real history is shaped by ideas.

This force is revealed in the interaction of the cognitive processes represented on stage. The sensitive audience recognizes, from that artistic experience, that the same principles demonstrated by great Classical art, are the principles by which peoples must shape the destiny of their nations. Thus, in this way, as the playwright and historian Friedrich Schiller defined the standard of competence for Classical tragedy, the audience must leave the performance of the Classical tragedy better, more insightful people, than had entered the theater a few hours earlier.

That is real politics, as practiced by the only people who are truly serious about the outcome of current history. That, conversely, is the political mission which supplies Classical forms of art its unique legitimacy, its moral purpose.

The real-life incident which I shall put on stage,

____

2. Lyndon H. LaRouche, Jr., "How to Save a Dying U.S.A.," ***EIR***, July 16, 1999.

____

3. i.e., those of Aeschylus, Sophocles, Shakespeare, and Schiller, most notably.

4. Or, in Classical musical compositions based on the notion of obliging the singing and instrumental voices to interact polyphonically in a *bel canto*-driven, well-tempered mode, the contrapuntal principle of inversion, combined with the voice-species registration, uses dissonance and register-shift, to force singing out of the monotony deemed appropriate for the oompah-band, into a relentlessly driving sense of true musical thorough-compositional development. To free music of the monotony of noun-ness, into a domain of living verbs. To force the singers to sing "between the notes" in this way.

here, occurred nearly fifty years ago, during the year 1950. This was during the closing years of a time of my occupation with, among other projects, a comparison of the treatments of the natural (i.e., *bel canto*) vocalization of the poetry of Johann Goethe, by such composers as Mozart, Beethoven, Schubert, and Hugo Wolf. Already, then, I sensed, more and more, that those composers understood the principle of composition of ideas within Goethe's poetry distinctly better than Goethe himself. Nonetheless, I had also come to know that Goethe was perhaps the most elegant composer of short Classical poetry in modern times, the one quickest and slickest to provoke in me a hilarious sense of truly Classical metaphor.

Therefore, in assessing Goethe's poetry insofar as I knew it, I compared him not only to Keats, Shelley, Heine, and Shakespeare; but, I also included the setting of short Goethe poems, as *Lieder*, by the composers Mozart, Beethoven, Schubert, and Hugo Wolf, masters of Classical poetic composition in their own right.[5]

It was an incident which occurred during that year, which prompted me to reach a certain crucial political conclusion, concerning a crippling epistemological defect which lurked behind the customary Classical elegance of Goethe's form of poetic composition.

The incident which then provoked my judgment to this effect, involved a poetic soliloquy, excerpted from the draft of one of Goethe's plays, a soliloquy which came to be recognized as the celebrated Goethe poem ***Prometheus***.[6] That soliloquy reflects the influence of the ideas of Classical artistic composition, those of Aeschylus, Sophocles, Plato, and Shakespeare, which Gotthold Lessing had revived in Germany. The crux of the discussion on this 1950s occasion, was the examination of the Goethe poem itself, within the setting of that soliloquy, ***Prometheus***, provided by the music critic and composer Hugo Wolf. Wolf's instinct for the musical side of vocalization of poetry often, happily, overwhelmed deliciously his factitious practice of musical Romanticism.

During 1950, I had been introduced to personal acquaintance with Vincent ________, and his wife, who had become known to me previously only from Vincent's reputation spilling over, as if from the other side of the fence, from a decade earlier, as having been a philosophical anarchist from Lynn, Massachusetts' circles of left-wing politics and poetry. During the period of the several occasions on which I was occasionally their guest, they were living in the quaint, celebrated Massachusetts fishing town of Gloucester, a few miles up the New England coast from Lynn.

This was during a time, my 1947-1952 years, when my activities included the occasional composition of poetry in the Classical mode, a preference which my host and I shared, but on which we differed. He was a true artist, and therefore expressed no difference with me on the principles of composition of poetry as such. Rather, the gist of his view on this account, was that the audience's current *Zeitgeist* required so-called progressive, modernistic forms. Differences, on both politics and poetry, made the discussions the more interesting; the fact that we were serious about ideas, in Plato's sense of ideas, made these occasional visits attractive, and fruitful encounters in respect to their by-products. As study of Plato should have taught each of you, disagreements over principle, situated in a pleasant social setting, have often been, for me, as for many others past and present, the most profitably stimulating grist for creative work.

In this setting, in one of the informal seminars held at Vincent's residence that year, it became my turn to contribute a theme. I brought up the subject on which I had been reflecting for some time: both the Classical idea of Prometheus, and, with it, both the Goethe poem and its Hugo Wolf setting. My reaction to the outcome of my presentation, and our discussion, on that occasion, contributed in a marginally significant way to shaping that approach to both science and Classical artistic composition, which was embodied within my subsequent, 1952, initial articulation of what were to become known world-wide, later, as the principles of the LaRouche-Riemann Method.

Sometimes, the correction of a seemingly small error, even a seemingly tiny error, if it involves a point

---

5. The use of the term *Lieder*, as distinct from the commonplace use of the same German word for song, is used here in the restricted sense of conformity to the form of well-tempered *bel canto,* polyphonic composition set into motion by Wolfgang Mozart's composition of ***Das Veilchen***. See, *A Manual on the Rudiments of Tuning and Registration,* Book I, (Washington, D.C.: Schiller Institute, 1992). One of the most celebrated discoveries of universal principle in music, was that of Mozart's reading of Bach's ***A Musical Offering***. Mozart's reading, and further development of a musical true metaphor in counterpoint, by Bach, in that work, led into the kind of compositional revolution in music toward which Haydn had been yearning in his Opus 33 string quartets. See, Lyndon H. LaRouche, Jr., "Norbert Brainin on Motivführung," *EIR*, September 22, 1995.

6. Johann Wolfgang Goethe, ***Prometheus: Dramatisches Fragment***, in **Werke**, Vol. 4, p. 176 (Munich: Deutscher Taschenbuch-Verlag, 1998).

of principle, can shape a great matter. So, as Carl Gauss showed for the case of the asteroid Ceres, a seemingly infinitesimal error in the Gauss-Riemann characteristic of Earth's orbit, would have been sufficient to doom our planet, long ago. The crucial importance of what might appear, mistakenly, as a mere subtlety of my understanding of the deeper importance of the Classical Greek conception of Prometheus, was forced upon my reflections during the weeks following the discussion which I had shared with my hosts and other participants in the informal seminar.

The participants in that seminar, had emphasized, that my rendering of the content of the Goethe poem, in English, was more successful artistically, than the Wolf setting.[7] I often recalled, later, how I was startled by that response. Over the following days, I thought about that criticism, and was soon satisfied that they were correct. After a well-prepared presentation of a subject, during a seminar among serious people, you may have reason to smile in acknowledgment of the fact, that you sometimes taught yourself more than you had taught the others.

The process of individual discovery, and refinement of one's own knowledge of universal principles, takes the form of a dialogue within one's self. It is the experience of that self-critical process of change, the which is generated by such internal dialogues, which should lead one to a more refined sense of one's inner self. Such a dialogue on some specific paradox, may be recurring over days, weeks, or longer. On one occasion, it is with others. On another occasion, it is with oneself. Nonetheless, on every occasion, it is always, primarily, with oneself.

It is one's insight into the process of change, associated with the outcome of repeated efforts to perfect such dialogues, through which one's private self-image is elevated. One may be transformed by such habits, away from the self-conception of a fixed thing, into a conception of oneself as a process of changing, a continuing process of becoming a better person. So, in Plato's *The Republic*, the leading figure, Socrates, argues for truthfulness and justice. It is in such experiences, and their outcome, that a truthful conception of the nature of both man and the universe is molded.

If ever this Socratic process of change of one's per-

ception of universal principle, for the better, ceases, it is for the body as if a certain kind of willful death of the soul has set in, after which that still-living, emptied body only passes time.

Just so, in my later reflections upon that evening's discussion, it dawned upon me, that, from the evidence contained within the internal features of that song, Goethe and Wolf, each in his own way, had expressed the wrong conception of the so-to-speak real-life Prometheus, and also of man.

A little less than two years after that discussion, I had occasion to put forth my corrected view on the subject of Goethe's *Prometheus*. About a year after that, I came to emphasize, that Brahms' setting of *I Corinthians* 13, in the conclusion of his *Four Serious Songs*, was a better poetic address to the actual issue posed by the Prometheus theme, and much better music. Both qualities had been achieved by Brahms without the epistemological flaw.

This reference to Brahms was prompted by my reflections upon a young baritone's, Dietrich Fischer-Dieskau's recorded presentation of the Brahms.[8] Reflections upon strongly motivated, repeated study of that recorded performance, implicitly confirmed some crucial features of the correction of my 1950 estimate respecting the poetic and musical answer to the problem posed by Goethe's *Prometheus*. I learned years later, and was not surprised by that report, that the greatest conductor of this century, Wilhelm Furtwängler, had had a hand in the polishing of young Fischer-Dieskau's performance of the Brahms.

How To Read a Poem

All this about a poem? As I shall demonstrate afresh, here, Shelley was right, when he proclaimed poets the true legislators for mankind.[9] To know the laws which govern the reshaping of the direction of history, you must know Classical poetry, as the point is illustrated by the sense of that discussion of *Prometheus*, in Gloucester, back in 1950.

As I have already forewarned you, do not allow yourself to be so small-minded, as to think that such cultural issues are relatively unimportant to the practical side of life in your community today. The fate of you

<hr>

7. For that occasion, I presented the recorded performance, using a eminently qualified singer, as supplied from the HMV pressings of the Hugo Wolf Society.

8. 8. Johannes Brahms, *Vier ernste Gesänge*, Op. 121, Dietrich Fischer-Dieskau (baritone) and Hertha Klust (piano), Decca DL9666 (1953). The recording has been re-released as part of the Deutsche Grammophon Centenary Collection CD 13, catalogue no. 459012.
9. op. cit.

Wilhelm Furtwängler, the greatest conductor of this century, emphasized, not the reading of the literal text of a composition, but "the music, the cognitive ironies which must not be buried under the mere text," LaRouche writes.

and your family might now depend upon your grasp of these issues.

The trouble is, very few people today, including most professional actors, know how to read a poem, such as the legislative work of Shakespeare's trage-dies.[10] Those with a formal university education in lit-erature and the arts, are perhaps not the worst, but usu-ally, like that poorer quality so painfully common among a large ration of today's technically proficient, professional musical performers, today's university graduates are the least likely to free themselves from foolish, pride-filled defense of their stubbornly adopted

---

10. His ***Richard III***, which Shakespeare based chiefly upon the docu-mentation of that crucial period of English history by Sir Thomas More, and his father before him, is key to understanding how the terrible Wars of the Roses were superseded by the conception of the modern sover-eign nation-state, pioneered in France by Louis XI, and introduced to England under Henry VII.

bad habits. Thus, the latter often prefer an interpretative reading of the literal text itself, rather than, as Furtwängler's conducting did, emphasizing the music, the cognitive ironies which must not be buried under the mere text.

Most public recitations of the poetry I love, drive me from the room, unless I am held there by loyalty to the efforts of a student's recitation, his, or her effort, thus, to learn what real poetry is. The performance of Shakespeare by most professional actors, disgusts me by its plain travesty! When such offenders de-liver such poetry, they are posturing for effect; their offense lies in the fact that they are not even seriously attempting to "put across" the contrapuntal play of ideas which is the subject of every good Classical poem produced.

The essence of all great Classical art-forms, is a polyphonic interweaving of ironies, metaphor. The essence of poetry, is, that words as such could not contain the meaning of ideas. Relative to any literal statement in words, no matter how sincerely those words are chosen, reality is always ambiguous: the mere words leave something impor-tant out. It is not the reality itself which is ambiguous; it is the literal use of words which is always false to reality. Classical art cor-rects the error, to bring the idea corresponding to reality into the mind of the hearer, where the mere literal words could not. In poetry, as in all Classical art, the artist uses ambiguities about the use of not only words, but com-monly known ideas, in order to impart to the mind of the hearer a sense of the reality which literal use of words could never accomplish.

In Classical sculpture, for example, the principle of ambiguity is the same. Thus, back in 1946, I was de-lighted by lectures on the work of the great Classical sculptors Scopas and Praxiteles, which made clear to me, how all Classical composition functions.

In contrast to the tombstone-like quality of Archaic forms of earlier Greek and Egyptian sculpture, Classi-cal sculpture captures a body in mid-motion, as if off balance. Thus, to the mind, the Classical sculpture ceases to be a mere symbolic work, but rather commu-

Sculpture by the Classical Greek sculptor Praxiteles of Hermes with the infant Dionysus. "In contrast to the tombstone-like quality of Archaic forms of earlier Greek and Egyptian sculpture, Classical sculpture captures a body in mid-motion, as if off balance."

nicates a sense of the body in mid-motion to the mind of the viewer. Thus, the ambiguity in the sculpture, is recognized by the mind as an image which is nearer to reality than the merely literal representations of inferior, symbolic representation.

It is most informative, to look at the way in which the same problem addressed by Classical sculpture appears in Classical Greek, as opposed to inferior Latin notions of space-time. The Roman conception, like that of Hobbes, Descartes, and Newton, is of a rectilinear universe of matter (objects) roaming in space and time. The ancient Greek Classical thinkers, such as Plato, looked at the physical universe as Scopas and Praxiteles defined Classical sculpture. The real universe, including the view by Classical Greek astronomy, was not seen as rectilinear in form, but as a curved universe, just as the angular measurements of the ancient astronomers defined the universe as a whole as a more or less spherical one.

The function of all Classical art is the same as that.

Literal meanings are always false to reality. It is through focussing upon the ambiguities posed by attempting to explain the world in terms of literal statements, that the human mind discovers the real universe hidden behind the deceptive screen of rectilinear-like, literal statements.

When the educated person recites a Classical poem atrociously, but apparently according to some academically accepted rule, he misses the purpose of art entirely.

In the case of Hamlet's much-celebrated Act Three soliloquy, "To be, or not to be...," the soliloquy addresses a conflict between two states of mind at war within the same person. Whether to cling to his present habits of behavior, which he knows will doom him and his nation, or, to leave the folly of his accustomed ways, for what is for him the unfamiliar alternative, the choice which might save him. He then pleads his excuses, his awe-stricken fear of the unfamiliar, and announces thus his intent to march to his doom. Thereafter, the audience follows his fateful decision to its natural outcome, his chosen doom.

Those are among the ironies of the drama; that is the metaphor, the idea of the tragedy of that Prince and his kingdom. That is what the poetry provides the actor the means to do: to put across to that audience, that idea, and its accompanying passions. On this point, most of the most famous actors fail miserably. They are so occupied with parading themselves on stage, that they leave the real poetry, the ideas, if they ever had them, behind, in the dressing room.

What must be imparted by the performance of a Classical tragedy, to the insight of the audience, is that stream of irony, whose subsuming metaphor is the idea to be conveyed by the reading of the poem. It is the same with music. In music, sight-reading is an indispensable capability, but when it is abused by the formally-trained user's temptation to sing and interpret the literal score of a worthwhile composition, as if symbolically, rather than the music, the result of public performance must be a saddening one.

The poor pedant never grasps the essence of either true science or Classical art. He resists the notion, that ideas do not reside within any literal language itself. All decent poetry is premised upon the principle of Ideas. All ideas, whether in science or Classical art, are metaphors, whose existence lies entirely outside any literal reading of language itself. The symbol-minded conceit, that one might cause the idea to appear, like a Genie from Aladdin's lamp, by stroking the spoken language of the poetry or musical score itself, is the rule of performance most likely to assure a pitiable sort of result, in any language, in any choice of artistic medium. The attempt to replace a lack of comprehension of the actual artistic idea, by some ruse of interpretive reading of the words, or notes, of the written text, is the practice, which like illiterate efforts of Roman sculptors to replicate Greek sculpture, is most likely to succeed in transforming a pitiably sterile, literal performance, into an vividly pathetic one.

Poetic ideas are generated, not from language, but, as Goethe did, or Keats, or Shelley, by absorbing the human cognitive processes' experience of the real world. As Dante Alighieri showed, art is generated, as the expression of those ideas, by forcing the language to dance, as it may be possible to force it to do so. Language must dance to the tune set within a domain of the mind into which language itself could never intrude. Indeed, one of the traditional auxiliary functions of Classical poetry, such as Dante's celebrated ***Commedia***, has been to transform the use and forms of expression within the language itself, for this very purpose.

Nonetheless, for all that, ideas are not the property of any language or custom. Ideas are imparted by the artist who has mastered the method of making his particular choice of language his obedient slave, as Dante did, as Goethe mastered this much, and more than a bit more.

The ideas of Classical European art are derived essentially from the Classical Greek notion of ideas as such. This is a notion expressed in the great art of the Golden Age of ancient Greece, and of Plato's Academy up through the time of Eratosthenes. Modern European Classical art, and every renaissance in European history, was built upon the foundation of replicating the same notion of ideas earlier stated in this Classical Greek.

The ideas themselves belong to none of those particular languages. None of them can be brought forth from within the language itself. It is the ideas, as they exist independently of the language used as a medium, which are the content and subject of art. It is as Dante Alighieri emphasized in his work, ideas which must shape language to their need, not permitting the mere current, vulgar, or other customs in use of language, to be imposed upon ideas.

It is this fact, that the idea rises above differences in spoken and written languages, which chances to empower Classical musical composition, since Johann Sebastian Bach, with a degree of immediate prescience of universality, which is not achieved in any other non-plastic medium.

Actual communication of ideas, including artistic conceptions, occurs as if directly from mind to mind, not as "information" embodied within some transmitted literal message. It is the image of an idea, existing in one mind, generated, and thus reproduced, within another mind, which is scientific and artistic communication of principled ideas. Artistry—and true scientific thinking—lies within the developed capacity to see, and also to cause others to see, an idea of this quality, as such, in its non-verbal, non-literal form, as an idea in its own right.[11]

In rule-of-thumb usages, we may refer to this capacity for direct communication among minds by indirect means, as "insight." True artistic composition begins with the non-literal idea in the mind of the composer; the words or notes are then selected as they seem, to the composer's mind, to fit the intent to evoke a corresponding generation of the same source-idea within the cognitive processes of another mind.

For example, if two actors rendering Shakespeare's celebrated Act Three Hamlet soliloquy, both proceed, independently, from a competent, cognitive comprehension of the same idea of both the play and soliloquy, that fact of such underlying agreement, will be recognizable to a sensitive audience, even if the specific style of delivery differs from one actor's presentation to the other's.

For example, conductor Furtwängler's conception of what is sometimes described as "performing between the notes" is so distinctive in its benefit to presenting the composer's idea, that, in earlier years, I have often recognized its distinctiveness on hearing even glimpses of his recorded conducting. This startlingly superior conducting, which I first recognized with astonishment on hearing an HMV recording of a Tchaikowsky symphony under his baton, in early 1946, evoked the same sensation as I later experienced in the first hearing of a Fischer-Dieskau performance of the "Four Serious Songs," especially the final song, during the early 1950s.

In music, otherwise, this is the singular quality which I later recognized in the work of the Amadeus Quartet, led by Primarius Norbert Brainin, and of out-

---

11. *Performing artistry*, as distinct from its essential basis found only in the artistry in the mind, lies in the development of the means to effect this expression with a certain degree of perfection.

The former Primarius of the Amadeus Quartet, Norbert Brainin. Describing the singular quality of his playing, LaRouche writes, "I have often referred to this as placing the emphasis on performing the 'verbs,' rather than the mere nouns."

standing other violinists in the Boehm-Joachim-Flesch-et al. tradition. It was much the same kind of distinction achieved by Pablo Casals, as both 'cellist and conductor. I have often referred to this as placing the emphasis on performing the "verbs," rather than the mere nouns.

Never permit the mere notes, or words, or a particular choice of language, to impose their will upon the process by which one person's mind prompts the generation of its idea from within the insightful mind of another person. Never do what I have often heard uninspired religious professionals do in their sermons: let the Romanticized, repeated, sensual mouthing of a noun chosen as the theme of the sermon, take over the occasion. True art never substitutes the fakery which is symbolism, for cognitive thinking.

Such issues are also the essence of the Classical-humanist method of education. It is the essence of com-munication in Classical artistic compositions. In contrast, the athletically well-trained musical performer, for example, like the modernist stage director, will follow the footsteps of Franz Liszt at his Romantic worst, to use sensual effects as a method of diverting the audience's attention away from the lack of actual artistic idea-content in either the performance, the composition itself, or both. Thus, the cognitively impaired performance, which is typical of the Romantic or modernist, aims, through symbolism, at the bestial passions of sense-perceptual experience, rather than reaching toward the human mind.[12]

Thus, the Romantic, modernist, or post-modernist composer or performer, often has one leaving the concert feeling that one has passed the evening listening to the singing of one who first learned to sing after he was dead, or, worse, perhaps, as in the case of modernists of the Frankfurt School of Theodor Adorno, never actually born. In such cases, the human feeling uniquely associated with cognitive insight, the cognitive resonance of the sound of the soul singing, is wanting.

So, as Mozart, Beethoven, and Schubert proved, and, Schiller, too, showed, they each understood the principles of musicality implied by Goethe's poetry, better than Goethe.[13] The same issue is that raised by Wilhelm Furtwängler, under the rubric of "reading between the notes."[14] This issue of the musicality of poetry, and of Classical forms of poetry, as the origin of all developments leading into the origins of music, is the point of reference from which I proceed here.

That view of the matter of reading a poem, or reproduction of a musical composition, defines the medium in which to situate the outcome of the discussion of **Prometheus**, the which occurred at Vincent _______'s residence.

---

12. Remember the old gag about the famous Bible-thumping, much "in your face" parson, who had died. When his zealous devotees used the occasion, to peek at last into that parson's celebrated, well-thumbed, much-pounded Bible, they often found repeatedly, in the words pencilled into the margin beside some heavily underlined portion of scripture, the phrase: "Meaning unclear: shout like Hell!"

13. See Chapter 11, "Artistic Beauty: Schiller versus Goethe," *A Manual on the Rudiments of Tuning and Registration*, op cit.

14. 14. See my fuller discussion of the superiority of Furtwängler's approach in the following locations: "What Economics Must Measure," *EIR*, November 28, 1997, p. 29; "The Comet of Doom," *EIR*, January 2, 1998, p. 37; "The Substance of Morality," *EIR*, June 26, 1998, pp. 31-32; and "Food, Not Money, Is the Crisis," *EIR*, November 13, 1998, pp. 36-38.

2. Three Views of Prometheus

The various, reasonably well informed, but conflicting appreciations of the Classical Greek image of the figure Prometheus, may be assorted among three broad moral classifications. This leads us toward a still more profound conception, one of great importance for understanding the crisis of extended European civilization worldwide, today. Bear in mind, that these three views of Prometheus are mutually opposing political views, representing, collectively, the standpoint from which the critical issues of politics, throughout modern European civilization, are to be understood, still today.

All views concur with the version which identifies that figure of Classical art, Prometheus, as an immortal, ranking among the gods and demi-gods. His offense was to teach human beings such forbidden arts as the use of fire, among the other technologies by means of which the human species might be able to save itself from the unpleasant destiny intended for it by the ruling gods of Olympus. Since the mythical Prometheus was, according to the sundry accounts, an immortal, the pagan gods could not kill him, but they submitted him to captivity and perpetual torture, instead. His refusal to capitulate to his captors, even under torture, was considered by the latter his greatest offense.

The first of the three contrasted views of Prometheus, is a morally repulsive one. To be specific, it is the reactionary conservative's view of Prometheus, as from an oligarchical standpoint. It is fairly summed up, as judging Prometheus as, either guilty of the crime of *hubris* against all of the pagan gods, or, as a tragic figure fallen victim to his own error of tactical indiscretion, of breaking the "club rules" of the oligarchical game.[15] That view includes the argument, that Prometheus, unlike Galileo, was guilty of refusing to make a reasonable submission to the authority of his tormentors.[16] On that, and other premises, Galileo is clearly not "my kind of person."

"*As Mozart, Beethoven, and Schubert proved, and, Schiller, too, showed, they each understood the principles of musicality implied by Goethe's poetry, better than Goethe.*"Shown here is a statue of Goethe (left) and Schiller at the German Cultural Garden in Cleveland, Ohio.

---

15. That has been the frequently expressed view of this writer among spokesman of the oligarchy. One leading member of the British-American-Canadian intelligence establishment made the point, immediately after my imprisonment: "He tried to make policy without having paid his dues, and for that he got the punishment he deserved." Such is the nature of the oligarchical "establishment" which has usurped our nation's powers of government today.

16. Thus, when true evidence of guilt of the accused is lacking, today's crooked Federal judges and prosecutors in the tradition of English Justice Jeffreys' Bloody Assizes, shift to trying their innocent victims for the alleged crime of insolence, the crime of being unwilling to confess, and repent.

The second view of Prometheus, which also appears as a mistaken reading of the Homeric character Ulysses, is the view of Prometheus as, perhaps a tragic figure shaking his angry fist, expressing thus a supposedly noble spirit of revolt, by the oppressed, against the bad gods. This is one permissible reading of Goethe's soliloquy as such, and is certainly Wolf's apprehension of Goethe's intent. This second was the view which prompted some contemporaries of Karl Marx as a young man, to portray him, inappropriately, as a Prometheus-figure.

The third view, which is introduced by Aeschylus' **Prometheus Bound**, defines the tyrant Zeus, not the hero Prometheus, as the tragic figure of the drama. Zeus is that tyrant and crooked judge whose beastly defiance of the immortal Prometheus brought doom, upon not only Zeus, but all of the gods of Olympus. It is this reading of Aeschylus' Prometheus trilogy,[17] upon which contemporary European republican opinion modelled its references to Benjamin Franklin as a "new Prometheus." They spoke of Franklin in terms of "God's sparks." The latter reference is that adopted so famously by Friedrich Schiller in his *An Die Freude*, and by Beethoven for his Ninth Symphony. This is also Schiller's pervasively implied conception of the Prometheus image itself.

The view presented by Aeschylus, as imperfectly echoed by Goethe's poem, was, for a time, my own, a view of Aeschylus' *Prometheus Bound* which I had adopted, largely, under the influence of Goethe himself. If one recalls the moral self-degradation into which most of my fellow-veterans sank during the half-dozen, cultural-pessimism-ridden, post-Roosevelt years, it might be recognized, that my reaction against that then-pervasive stench of cultural pessimism, influenced the reading I tended to project upon the Goethe poem. Although that projected view erred only by virtue of what might be misread as a very small margin, since that error involved a matter of principle, it included a critical error of principle, even if a humanly understandable error. Until the aftermath of the referenced evening at Vincent's, the still deeper, nobler implications of the Prometheus image had not yet been brought home to me.

Had we today the last two, mostly lost parts of Aeschylus' *Prometheus* trilogy, the deeper implications of the Prometheus theme would, doubtless, be more widely understood, studied against the background of Aeschylus' own sometimes perilous relationship to the irate keepers of the Eleusinian mysteries.[18] Lacking the lost parts, we must place the greater responsibility upon other evidence, in our searches into the meaning of the continuing, deep relationship between the Prometheus image and the political history of European civilization.

If, as I shall show, the Prometheus image is of such crucial importance in the political history of extended European civilization, still today: What is the historical and artistical truth of the matter? Who, if anybody, was the real-life Prometheus, and what is the specific nature of the importance of this issue for current history? *What is the validatable universal principle of politics involved?*

On that account, I reference several sets of evidence here. First, there are chronologies in which various ancient reporters situated their real-life Prometheus. Second, there is the critical, scientific reading of those chronologies, the first that of Plato, the second my own. Finally, there is the view which overlaps my appreciation of Plato's work as a whole, including his celebrated *Timaeus*, which looks at Christianity and its legacy, as the location in which the role of the Prometheus image must be situated for comprehension of the principles *which are demonstrated by the transition of the Mediterranean region, from ancient times, into the emergence and development of modern European civilization as such.*

The obvious chronologies, include those referenced by Plato and those of Diodorus Siculus,[19] as these might be compared with the work of Herodotus.[20] Taken together, all these chronologies, tell us a story. We must listen to the narrators of the chronicles with what Theodore Reik, for example, identified as our "third ear."[21] Is the story truthful? Is the account attributed to the ancient Egyptian authority Manetho, to be taken as factual?

When these accounts are situated circumstantially, within the hard evidence bearing on the broadest physical and closely related features of the recent 12,000-odd years of life in the Mediterranean region, we are confronted by a case of alarming verisimilitude.

First, summarize the chronologies, which run to the following effect.

About 12,000 years ago, or somewhat earlier, a flotilla of ships arrived from the Atlantic Ocean, to found a colony in the region of modern Morocco, near the Straits of Gibraltar, in the vicinity of the Atlas Mountains. The colonists found there a relatively primitive culture, that of the ancient Berbers, whom the colonists educated in methods of agriculture, and made subjects of the colony. After a time, the sons of a royal concubine, Olympia, conspired to murder the tyrannical ruler, and seize power for themselves. The leading figure

---

17. Only fragments of the later two parts survive today.

18. Location of Aeschylus' family origins, and the center of the oligarchy expelled from Athens by the great republican reforms of Solon. The mysteries, which Aeschylus was seen as betraying, are among the relevant topics to be included in understanding Aeschylus' Prometheus trilogy.

19. *Diodorus Siculus*, Volumes 1 and 2, Loeb Classical Library (Cambridge, Mass.: Harvard University Press).

20. *Herodotus: The Histories* (London: Penguin Books Ltd., 1996).

21. Reik was a prominent U.S. immigrant and psychiatrist, whose emphasis on the point was presented in his book, *Listening with the Third Ear: The Inner Experience of a Psychoanalyst* (New York: Farrar, Strauss, Giroux, 1948).

among these revolting sons of Olympia, was Zeus.

Prometheus was one of the legitimate heirs to the power of the colony. He joined the Olympians in the opposition to the tyranny itself, but fought against the brutalizing new tyranny which the patricidal sons of Olympia imposed upon the Berber population, over the corpse of Zeus's butchered father.

This occurred within the same, Peoples of the Sea, colony of the Atlas region, which extended its cultural impact throughout the Mediterranean littoral, to the included effect of participating in the founding of Egypt at a time now about 10,000 years ago.

Once we recognize, despite British frauds over the subject of "linear B," and so on, that the populations of the period of Greece prior to its usually referenced "dark age," were the same "Greeks" who had, as Peoples of the Sea, populated that area, and Cyrenaica, as elsewhere, during the millennium preceding that "dark age," we begin to close the gap between 12,000 B.C. and the emergence of Ionian sea-power as rivals to Phoenician maritime power. If we take into account some great catastrophe, perhaps a natural catastrophe, which wiped out much of the culture pre-existing about 10,000 B.C., the conceptual gap between 12,000 and 600 B.C., if not the actual lapse of time, shrinks. We may view this interval of nearly 10,000 years, as knowledgeable people today think of the Norman Conquest, Charlemagne, the birth of Christ, the great dynasties of ancient Egypt, and Vedic astronomers in Central Asia during the interval between 6,000 and 4,000 B.C.

The legacy of these events in the ancient Atlas region, and the policy-fight between Prometheus and the Olympians, persisted so, somehow, over the intervening millennia, to emerge as the pagan mythology of Olympus, as reflected in such places as the Homeric epics.

Such, in summation, is the chronicle and its setting.

Is that account a plausible one? First of all, the worst thing which can be said about it, is that, in no way does it appear to conflict with what is presently known. It corresponds in its adducible internal characteristics, and circumstantially, to the long existence, over millennia, of the cultural phenomenon known to early historical times as "Peoples of the Sea."

Secondly, most of the argument against the possibility of such a history, stems from the unfortunately widespread influence of what are known to have been academic frauds, concocted, chiefly, by Eighteenth- and Nineteenth-century British hoaxsters. Those known frauds, include the absurdity, foisted by so-called "Biblical archeologists," and others, which claimed that not only the world's civilization, but also the existence of the human species, began in Mesopotamia after 4004 B.C. Similarly, these hoaxsters shifted the actual dating of Egypt's history several thousand years closer to the present, as a way of defending claims for planet-wide, Mesopotamian precedence.

Contrary to the British monarchy's habit, in its adopted tradition of the Code of Diocletian, of encouraging its dupes not to think, there is relatively massive evidence of sophisticated human cultures existing in Europe 50,000 years ago, and crucial physical evidence, from European sites, showing evidence of human behavior as early as 400,000 years—the corresponding number of ice-age cycles—ago. There is also evidence of some devastating crisis throughout the Mediterranean region, or more widely, about 10,000 B.C., as well as awesome seismic events, such as the explosion of Thera, during the later period leading into the prolonged "dark age" of Greek civilization.

Consider the fact, that there is much evidence of a high degree of cultural development of solar astronomical calendars, and the languages related to those calendars, prior to the melting-phase of the last great glaciation in the northern hemisphere. This is part of the evidence pointing to the dominant role of transoceanic, especially transAtlantic, transPacific, and Indian Ocean maritime cultures, prior to the present interglacial period.

Consider the fact, of the rising of the relative levels of the seas and oceans by as much as 300-400 feet, sometimes at catastrophic rates, sometimes with accompanying, massive deluges, between the onset of the melting phase of the last ice-age and the present level reached about 2,000 years ago. This is to be taken into account in respect to those coastal sites of relatively denser, and higher levels of quality among some populations.

These circumstances thus reflect developments during the period since approximately 50,000 B.C., until 12,000 years ago, or even a later point of catastrophic climatic, seismic, and related crises afflicting what had been the most technologically advanced cultures of the immediately preceding times. Not only the rising of sea-levels, but also the effects of climate changes, in North Africa, Central Asia, and so forth, as a result of the unfolding of the present interglacial interval, are also to be emphasized, in looking back to the cultures which existed between 12,000 and 2,000 years ago.

Also take into account, the fact, that the Medieval falsehoods, which taught that the world is flat, or that the Sun orbits the Earth, were inherited by Medieval and modern Europe as intentional frauds. These had been introduced, as enforced delusions, to late-Hellenistic Europe under the culturally depraved influence of the Roman Empire. Such was but one of the many cultural calamities which Medieval and early Modern European culture suffered, despite contrary efforts of Christianity, from the legacy of what Christians of that time knew as "the New Babylon."

For those who know the actual circumstances of Christopher Columbus's rediscovery of America, this occurred as a by-product of the reopening, by leading Fifteenth-Century scientists associated with Cardinal Nicholas of Cusa, of the previously known feasibility, as by Eratosthenes of Egypt, of circumnavigation of the planet. Columbus' voyage was the direct result of the rediscovery, by Cusa's circles, of the sane astronomy which emerged from a long "dark age" imposed by the legacy of Roman culture. Take into account the fact, that European civilization today, is still suffering cultural disorders introduced to the eastern Mediterranean's civilization 2,200 years ago, a cultural catastrophe which began about the time of the Roman butchery of the great Archimedes.

The notion, that the cult of Olympus has an historic basis in fact, and the myth of Prometheus, too, is a much more probable view of the indicated chronologies, than any cuckoo hatched under the wings of the modern British monarchy. The ambiguities left unresolved by the foregoing types of evidence, may be cleared away by adducing the principle which underlies the pattern of transformations in the Greek view of gods and men, over the thousand of years or so preceding the missions of such Christian Apostles as John and Paul. Thus, in the end, we are advised to conceive the historical significance of the Prometheus image through the prism of Brahms' "Four Serious Songs."

Permit me to remind you again. Do not allow yourself to be so small-minded, as to think that such spans of cultural ties over many thousands of years, are relatively unimportant to the practical side of life in your local community today.

How Men See Their Gods

Look at the images of the pagan gods of Mesopotamia, or of ancient Egypt. These were gods portrayed in the Archaic, tombstone-like images of something worse than beasts. Contrast these proffered Mesopotamian and Egyptian deities, in the forms of beasts or polymorphs, to the all-too-human gods of Olympus, as these appear in the Homeric epics, and, appear again, as viewed differently in the tragedies of Aeschylus and Sophocles. Then, consider Plato's insistence, upon putting the issues posed by the great tragedians, on a still higher level, that of Plato's *Timaeus*, for example. Finally, look at the Classical Greek culture of Plato, as the Apostles John and Paul viewed this.

It can be said, from the vantage-point of Christianity, that, as a matter of a general rule, man imagines his gods according to a conception of the universe which coheres, functionally, with man's image of himself. As the monstrosities of Mesopotamian theology forewarn us, the image of the gods is not, as a rule, a symbol-minded sophist's projection of the image of man; it is invariably a reflection of man's image of the universe within which man dwells as a subject of that which he imagines to be the ruling power. The characteristic mapping of the relationship of the gods to men, within the Homeric epics, as in contrast to the view of the Classical tragedian Aeschylus, and both in contrast to the view of Plato, underscores the point.

The question thus posed is, which image of God, if any, is a truthful expression of that latter principle of ruling power?

Herein lies, without doubt, the significance of the Prometheus image. Aeschylus' Prometheus did not simply defy the pagan gods; he pointed toward a real God, the same God identified in Plato's *Timaeus*, upon whose justice for mankind Prometheus implicitly relied. The evidence is conclusive, that a Prometheus image was, artistically, a necessary idea, which contributed an essential role during the recent thousands of years of emergence of the best features of modern European civilization today. That is the more easily proven of two facts.

The more difficult question, whether an actual, historical Prometheus, more or less cohering with such an image, ever existed, must be judged from determining whether or not a person corresponding to that image *necessarily should have existed*. It will be useful, as you shall soon learn, that, for our strategic purposes here, we should focus upon the second question first.

As Herodotus should be heard, and the role of the Islamic Renaissance's ibn Sina should be read, the fact is, that what is often regarded today as the land-locked Indian subcontinent did, at various intervals, play a powerful role in the development of European civilization. The role of the ancient Dravidian maritime culture in founding civilization in lower Mesopotamia, is but one instance. Nonetheless, even after such considerations are taken into account, the development of European civilization over the recent three thousand years, during which Classical art of Scopas, Praxiteles, Leonardo da Vinci, and Raphael Sanzio, superseded the Archaic sculpture of Egypt and earlier Greece, represents a functionally distinct phase-space within the emergence of modern history world-wide.

Our focus here is upon that phase-space, and on certain circumstances, and validatable universal principles, which clearly exerted an impact of exceptional significance in that process. *The image of Prometheus contributed a necessary political, artistic principle to creating that phase-space. There is only one way in which this cultural phase-space can be defined: in*

An archaic Egyptian statue of god-as-beast. "It can be said, from the vantage-point of Christianity, that, as a matter of a general rule, man imagines his gods according to a conception of the universe which coheres, functionally, with man's image of himself."

terms of an emerging conception of the nature of man, a nature defined, functionally, in terms of man's willfully changing ability to change the relationship of the universe to ourselves. The conception of man implicit in the third perception of the Prometheus myth, is the crucial point on which to focus.

For reasons emphasized in an earlier report, this is the only way in which competent judgments as to principle, can be adduced in a way consistent with the requirements of proof. As specified there, the proof of any hypothetical universal principle, whether a physical principle, or one of Classical art, must meet the Riemannian standard of a *unique experiment*.[22] The only means by which this requirement can be satisfied, respecting the universal artistic principles reflected in man's changing the relationship of the universe to the human species, is the empirical standpoint embodied within my approach to a science of physical economy.

For related reasons, the matter of the Prometheus conception figured as a crucial element in my initial development of my contributions to that branch of physical science. In return, that branch of physical science enables us to unravel some of the mystery attached to the two questions I have underlined above.

From what we know with certainty today, the increase of the potential relative population-density of any past or present culture, is defined, as a movable upper limit, by a culture's submission to self-government by certain validatable kinds of universal principles. At the outside, these limits are defined by universal physical principles. Yet, the fostering of the discovery and employment of those physical principles, is shaped by those kinds of validatable universal principles typi-

---

22. Lyndon H. LaRouche, Jr., "How to Save a Dying U.S.A.," ***EIR***, July 16, 1999.

fied by the principles of Classical artistic composition.

Mankind's physical power in the universe, is a matter of actions taken according to valid, universal physical principles. However, the ability to discover those physical principles, and, also, the ability of society to cooperate in use of those discovered principles, depends upon principles which are unique to the human mind itself. The principles of Classical artistic composition are the form in which the principles of discovery and cooperation are preserved and taught.

In physical science, we are prompted to discover new, validatable universal physical principles by means of ambiguities arising in those unsuccessful attempts to explain reality, which arise because of the errors inhering in literal statements borrowed from currently accepted general classroom principles of mathematical physics. These ambiguities are identical in form to the true ambiguities of great Classical artistic compositions. Just as the Classical poet uses the principle of metaphor to prompt an hypothetical solution to that metaphor by the sovereign, creative cognitive processes of the individual mind, so the scientific discovery generates the validatable hypothesis which becomes a new universal physical principle. In sharing such a latter discovery with another mind, the scientific discoverer employs the same methods of cognitive interaction which define the relationship between the great artist and his audiences.

Thus, the principles of Classical Humanist education, are an expression of the same principles as met in Classical art. Without those latter principles which are best represented in the form of Classical artistic compositions—such as great Classical tragedy—a progressive form of civilized cooperation in society would not be possible. The transmission of valid discoveries of universal physical principle, from one generation to the next, depends upon methods of education which are identical with the principles of Classical artistic composition. Scientific progress would not be possible without those principles best known to us in the forms of Classical artistic composition.

Here lies the unique debt of the whole of extended European civilization to the Greek classic. Here is the key to the uniqueness of that European phase-space which was generated from precisely these Classical-Greek contributions to the foundations of science and Classical artistic composition.

The pinnacle of that contribution of ancient Greek civilization to modern civilization is that notion of the *idea*, as expressed in stone by Scopas and Praxiteles, the notion as made transparent by the dialogues of Plato. The kernel of this Classical Greek notion of the nature of the *idea*, is expressed as the impact of the Prometheus myth.

My specific contributions to science, as expressed by the LaRouche-Riemann Method, lie precisely here. See the Prometheus myth from the standpoint embodied in my discovery. It is, thus, in my work to that end, that it has become possible to show the necessity for the existence of an historical model for the Prometheus of Aeschylus.

Science as Art

The entirety of physical science depends upon correlating the knowledge developed, essentially, from the standpoint of study of four distinct areas of empirical inquiry: astronomy, microphysics, the distinction between living and non-living processes, and the distinction between the human species and all other living processes.

The first known science was the development of solar astronomical calendars. This had achieved the level of rather precise measurements of such long-term phenomena as equinoctial cycles long before the Dravidians established the first rudiments of civilization, Sumer, in lower Mesopotamia. In tandem with this development of early astronomy, there was transoceanic navigation based in such astronomy. From such foundations in construction of solar astronomical calendars, ancient Egypt and other locations provided the foundations, upon which ancient Greeks founded what developed into the foundations for the modern European science launched by Cardinal Nicholas of Cusa.

It was these foundations which provided us the notion of universal physical principles, principles associated with a notion of measurement itself rooted in the angular measurements of astronomy, as the premise for a notion of measurable regular curvature, and with this the notion of universal laws inherited by physics in general. The work of one of Cusa's and Leonardo da Vinci's successors, Johannes Kepler, provided what became the link to modern physics and microphysics, as Leibniz's concept of *monadology* led his followers to the notion of elementary forms of regular curvature of action in the microphysically small.

Ironically, although we have yet to define an absolute physical difference between the nature of what can be clinically distinguished as living and non-living processes, the work of Classical Greece had already bequeathed us the foundations for a rigorous, absolute notion of the functional distinction between human and other living processes. This distinction, as defined in spite of such hoaxsters as Immanuel Kant, is the notion of cognition, as the content of what we have defined here as both Classical artistic principles, and universal physical principles.

On the premises just stated, a simply biological distinction between man and higher ape, as biology is defined today, is virtually impossible. The only valid standard for human life, is evidence which bears upon the presence of human cognitive activity, as distinct from the lower capability which we share with lower animal life, the capability for learning, as chimpanzees, for example, do.[23]

The case of a report by Thieme,[24] implicitly dating the existence of human activity in Germany, to as early as 600,000 B.C., is exemplary. In this case, the crucial evidence involves throwing spears found in a site so dated. The design of these spears was based upon principles of design, therefore the product of cognition, rather than animal-like powers, of even human beings, for mere learning. Similarly, the evidence of the controlled and task-oriented use of fire in certain archeological sites, shows the product of human cognition, rather than mere learning. The discovery of datable cave-paintings which qualify as actual art, rather than crude symbolic images, often demonstrates the antiquity of humanity to prehistoric datings in the order of somewhere between 50,000 and 100,000 years.

The human species, as defined by modern man's distinction from the beasts, has lived on this planet for perhaps a million years, or even much more. Our species not only lived here already long ago, but did not exactly waste all that intervening prehistoric time. Cultures were developed, and even, no later than tens of thousands of years ago, what we would classify, without exaggeration, as art. Millions of years of solar-orbit-determined glacial cycles, and their effects, have obscured most of the physical traces of human exis-

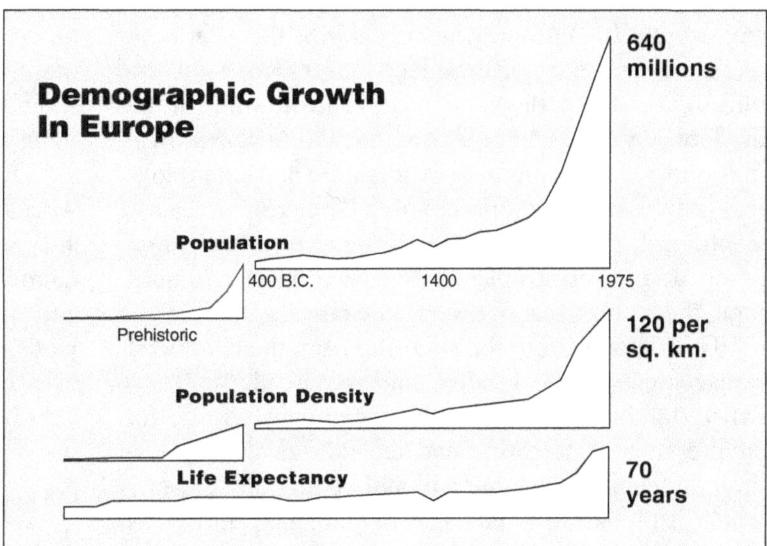

tence deep into pre-historic millennia, but we can infer certain among the incontestible, beneficial effects of the human cultures bequeathed to us from the lost shards of those earlier cultures.

When we look at the distinguishing characteristics of human populations over long periods, we are confronted by the phenomenon of increases of *potential relative population-density*, as I have defined that term.[25] [**Figure 1**.] This shows the effect of a fundamental distinction of the human species from all lower forms of life. That long-term view shows us two most significant general facts. First, man is the only species which has been able to willfully increase, successively, what I have defined as its potential relative population-density. Second, the greatest rate of such increase has been a product of the cultural changes introduced into and by European civilization beginning the great, Golden Renaissance of the mid-Fifteenth Century.

Looking at those two facts more closely, it is the establishment of a cultural-political revolution, the institution of the sovereign form of modern nation-state, beginning with France under Louis XI, which has been the source of that fostering of scientific and technological progress, out of which the recent centuries' acceleration of increase of potential relative population-density, was generated.

---

23. Thus, although Immanuel Kant claimed to be human, he, as the central point of Kant's *Critiques*, like his followers, defined himself, categorically, as not a cognitive being, and therefore not human.

24. Hartmut Thieme, "Lower Paleolithic Hunting Spears from Germany," *Nature*, Feb. 27, 1997, pp. 807-810.

25. e.g. Lyndon H. LaRouche, Jr., *So, You Wish To Learn All About Economics?*, second edition, (Washington, D.C.: EIR News Service, 1995).

There are some notable exceptions to that happier trend. World Wars I and II have proven a demographic catastrophe for Europe generally. Since the aftermath of the assassination of President John F. Kennedy, the willful, top-down, destruction of the institutions of the modern sovereign nation-state, including the willful uprooting of the promotion of scientific and technological progress, has produced both a demographic catastrophe in Europe, North America, and elsewhere, and an economic catastrophe among what had been, until then, the world's leading economic powers.

This downward trend, resulting from the combined replacement of the modern nation-state through so-called "globalization," and the accompanying, willful suppression of scientific and technological progress, now threatens to become a global demographic catastrophe, a global "new dark age" of humanity, perhaps as catastrophic as that which struck the Mediterranean region, in particular, during some time after 10,000 B.C.

Call these combined effects "The Catastrophe of the Twentieth Century." It is also known by other names. During much of this passing century, it was referred to by its utopian advocates as "The New Age," or "The Dawning of the Age of Aquarius." During the post-Kennedy 1960s, it became widely known as the "cultural paradigm-shift" of the "rock-drug-sex counterculture," and also proclaimed as either "the technetronic society" by Zbigniew Brzezinski, or, as a utopian "post-industrial society" more commonly.

This lunacy produced the 1972 launching of the world-wide "environmentalist" conspiracy, in furtherance of the aims of the World Wildlife Fund and "1001 Club" co-founded in 1961 by Prince Philip of England and Nazi SS veteran Prince Bernhard of the Netherlands. This produced such dangerous military lunacies of Newt Gingrich, Al Gore, and the Tofflers as "The Third Wave" and "Air-Land Battle 2000." It produced the programs leading into the recent Littleton horror, too.

What you behold in these catastrophic Twentieth-Century developments, is a real-life re-enactment of Aeschylus' **Prometheus Bound**. The modern version of a self-styled "gods of Olympus," centered around the Anglo-American-Canadian-Dutch oligarchy, has demanded the suppression of a real-life Prometheus, the suppression of the principle of betterment of the general condition of mankind, through fostering those kinds of cultural institutions which, in turn, ensure the benefits of scientific and technological progress. That today, has become the only war worth our fighting, a war to bring to an end the tyranny of such evil, would-be gods, the twilight of the gods. Let our courage, like that of Aeschylus' Prometheus, bring about the effect known as "the twilight of the gods." That result could not come too soon for humanity at large.

My contributions to the science of physical economy, have the specific historic importance, of showing, for the first time, how universal cultural principles must necessarily dominate the development of scientific and technological progress in effecting the improvement of the conditions of mankind as a whole.

When I, so to speak, came on the scene, it had become customary opinion, especially in the universities, to adopt the neo-Kantian irrationalism of Germany's Nineteenth-Century reactionary, Savigny, in insisting upon the absolute separation of physical science from art and statecraft. Kant's and Savigny's lunatic folly of "art for art's sake," reigned, both in the arts as such, and in politics. Classical art was in the process of becoming lost art. Populations were becoming increasingly irrational.

Then, it became worse. Since the anti-science "cultural paradigm-shift" of the late 1960s was introduced to the U.S.A., both art and science rapidly lost their grip on the new generations of university graduates, and the society as a whole became more and more irrational, and self-destructive, each year. To any typical American or European visitor arriving by time-capsule from the late Nineteenth Century, or even the close of World War II, the world of the past thirty years' trends "makes no sense."

When we consider what we know today, of both history and pre-history in the large, we should be warned against the popular delusion of something like an irrational "invisible hand" in the shaping of human existence as a whole. Without the recurring intervention of the virtual Prometheuses of both historic and pre-historic times, the human race would have gone nowhere, except, as now, toward its own destruction at the hand of forces such as either its own children, or the oligarchical "Olympian gods" of past and present times. The kind of creativity and dedication represented by the mythical Prometheus is an indispensable factor in the progress, even the survival of the human species.

Looking at the broad-brush features of ancient Greece's history and legacy, all that occurred for the better within that culture, was of a pro-Promethean quality. When we trace the emergence of the role of cognition in society, from the Homeric epics, through the Classical period, through Plato, and when we look at that result through the eyes of the Apostles John and Paul, or Augustine later, we recognize the specific importance of the idea of Prometheus as a special element of importance within the legacy of Greek culture, the element which sparked that culture into producing the foundations upon which all the best of modern European culture depends.

Somewhere in the pre-history shrouded by the millennial mists of the melting glaciation, there was a real Prometheus, by whatever name he were known in those times. Without some concretization of a Promethean tradition, resisting the deadening effects of a parasitical, Olympus-style oligarchy, Ancient Greece could not have achieved its unique role in generating Classical culture, and with it, the foundations on which Cusa and others based the emergence of modern European science.

In that sense, a Prometheus had necessarily existed. This was clear to me from reflecting on what I had discovered.

During adolescence, when I had adopted Leibniz, and recognized the importance of discrediting Kant, I had already understood the principle of cognition, as distinct from the dead hand of formal logic. In the immediate post-war period, when I was startled by my recognition of the danger to civilization embedded in Norbert Wiener's promotion of the radical-positivist notion of "information theory," I returned to my earlier upholding of Leibniz against Kant. In my concern to define cognition for the specific purpose of pointing out the fraud of "information theory," I chose the subject of Classical artistic composition as the way of demonstrating how the idea of cognition itself can be shared among persons.

Once we recognize that the physical profitability of production comes from a continuing factor of technological progress, and know the connection between the experiments proving a scientific principle and the generation of new technologies from that experiment, the general picture is clear.

Reflections on Immortality

However, this required an additional step. How do we define scientific and technological progress as a whole from the standpoint I had adopted respecting the relationship between Classical art and discovery of physical principle? Riemann supplied the key to solving that problem. But, then, another final step remains. The Riemannian edifice I assembled worked. The question was, what motivated that assembly into action? *Why should we—anyone—choose to progress in this way?*

What motivates us, as individuals, and groups of individuals, to devote our sense of identity to such work? The Apostle Paul's *I Corinthians* 13 supplies the gist of the answer: Plato called it *agapē*, a term which survives as a mere, commonly misunderstood English translation, as "charity." It is, as Prometheus was charged by Zeus: love of mankind, rather than what is called today "the establishment."

Now, state that same point a bit differently.

What quality must a person have, to be able to sustain that love of mankind in such a fashion, even when under the pain of immortal torture by the ruling oligarchy? Who would not play the contemptible, doomed role of a Hamlet under such fearful threat? Who would die, rather than recant and desist, as moral weaklings always do?

The answer lies within the domain of cognition itself. If we can see ourselves as we are, then we know that our mortal life is a talent given to us to spend in a way that the benefit we contribute shall be greater than that we have been given. When we recognize that the improvement of the condition of mankind, morally as physically, depends upon an endless stream of additions of newly discovered valid universal principles, of both Classical art and physical science, to the stock of mankind's power within and over the universe, our best hope for our brief mortal life is to add something of durable value to the mankind which comes after us.

Once that sense of one's proper true identity is acquired, you have the necessary motive to act as you must, to become the kind of person who can confront mortality with a smile. Anyone who has achieved that correct understanding of his, or her most vital personal self-interest, will not think differently about such matters than I do.

The trouble is, people who are not certain that their existence is really of any value to mankind, settle for lesser, even foolish questions, such as "I am too busy taking care of my family, my personal interests, and my community, to be bothered with such things. First things first!" Such small-minded people are the most foolish among the fooled people to whom President Lincoln referred.

Out of the parting mists of Mediterranean pre-history, came the necessary idea of Prometheus, the idea which sparked the birth of what became European civilization. People with such ideas, must win, in some way or another.